COLLECTED POEMS

By Horace Gregory

POETRY

Chelsea Rooming House
No Retreat
Chorus for Survival
Poems 1930–1940
Selected Poems
Medusa in Gramercy Park
Alphabet for Joanna

PROSE

Pilgrim of the Apocalypse:
    A Study of D. H. Lawrence
The Shield of Achilles:
    Essays on Beliefs in Poetry
A History of American Poetry Since 1900
    (in collaboration with Marya Zaturenska)
Amy Lowell:
    Portrait of the Poet in Her Time
The World of James McNeill Whistler
The Dying Gladiators and Other Essays

TRANSLATIONS

The Poems of Catullus
Ovid's Metamorphoses
Love Poems of Ovid

EDITOR

New Letters in America
The Triumph of Life:
    An Anthology of Devotional and Elegiac Verse
The Portable Sherwood Anderson
The Snake Lady and Other Stories of Vernon Lee
Selected Poems of Robert Browning
    (Rinehart Editions)
The Mentor Book of Religious Verse
    (in collaboration with Marya Zaturenska)
The Crystal Cabinet:
    An Invitation to Poetry
        (in collaboration with Marya Zaturenska)

Horace Gregory

COLLECTED POEMS

HOLT, RINEHART AND WINSTON

NEW YORK   CHICAGO   SAN FRANCISCO

Designer: Ernst Reichl

83277–0614

Printed in the United States of America

FOR
MARYA ZATURENSKA

Prefatory Note

The present collection contains all I wish to keep of six books of poems. Therefore this book is slightly less in the number of pages than the total of the six which came before it.

With few exceptions, the poems reappear in chronological order, yet a number of them have been retouched, and this was done in the interest of deeper clarity and sharpness of meaning. Seven of them, "A Wreath for Margery" and poems "Eight" through "Twelve" in *Chorus for Survival* as well as the lines with their new title, "The Door in the Desert," are very close to being entirely new poems, and the better, I think, for what they mean to say. Another change is in the transference of a monologue from *Chorus for Survival* to *The Passion of M'Phail*, a later group of poems. Actually the monologue (without my knowing it then) anticipated the tone of voice, the spirit of McPhail in whose speech it has now found its proper relevance. From my not very distant past these poems re-emerge with altered shades of meaning in the present.

Because the neighborhood where *Chelsea Rooming House* was first conceived has gone the way of urban transformations, perhaps the monologues of my first book demand a word or two of descriptive commentary. The monologues were scarcely autobiographical at all. They were of New York and its people from a Chelsea vantage point, a view that was bounded by the West River docks and a stretch of "Hell's Kitchen"; on the east by Fifth Avenue; on the south by Greenwich Village; on the north by the garment industries and trade. Within this area rose the dark pile of the Chelsea Hotel, where Dickens once stayed on a visit to the United States, and north and west of it were brownstone fronts called "Suicides' Row." On nearby avenues and streets were scattered maroon and oak-walled Irish-American saloons where "needled beer" was served. Farther north and west was the French garden restaurant where John Butler Yeats, the poet's father, dined and talked the nights away. There were also white-tiled all-night lunch rooms where, when on nights I could not sleep, I drank a four-in-the-morning cup of coffee. Aside from these was the charming white stone façade of what had once been Lily Langtry's house, whose street floor had been converted into a "Beauty Parlor" from which a yellow-wigged, brightly pink wax head stared through a plate-glass window. From there, and to the north and west again, stood the tall, narrow, dignified though moth-eaten, stone-fronted mansion that housed the offices of *The New Republic*, and to the east and south, a block of battered, century-old red brick buildings that had "Rooms to Let."

The people who walked the streets of Chelsea were the strays of the city. They were ex-circus performers, ex-Boston-Irish, ex-Broadway actors—ex-everything that one could think of, all figures of nightmare who seemed to find cheerful pride in their distress. In particular, there was a six-foot beggar with a great round smiling face who carried a rusty sword and wore the torn remains of a Confederate Civil War uniform. These were not I: yet I held before me the examples set by Hardy's compassionate *Satires of Circumstance*. It so happened that the creatures I overheard and saw around me held portents of human waste, bewilderment, and loss that were so deeply and generally felt during the decade before World War II. I feel that some of these sources of inspiration did not play false. Whatever their flaws, the monologues of *Chelsea Rooming House* remain very nearly as I wrote them in the seven years preceeding 1930.

The poems now appearing under the general titles *Fortune for Mirabel* and *The Door in the Desert* were originally published in my *Poems 1930–1940* (1941) and *Selected Poems* (1951). Among the earlier group, "Two Letters from Europe" probably requires brief annotation. The poems were written soon after the beginning of World War II—which I assume is clear enough. Less clear perhaps are the references to Søren Kierkegaard's *Fear and Trembling* in the first letter, and to Euripides' *Iphigenia in Aulis* in its last line; also, in the second letter, there are references to the legendary figure of Goethe, who reappears later in the volume.

—H.G.

Contents

Medusa in Gramercy Park (1961), 159

CHELSEA
ROOMING HOUSE

(1930)

FOR MARYA AND JOANNA

Longface Mahoney Discusses Heaven

If someone said, Escape,
let's get away from here,
you'd see snow mountains thrown
against the sky,
cold, and you'd draw your breath and feel
air like cold water going through your veins,
but you'd be free, up so high,
or you'd see a row of girls dancing on a beach
with tropic trees and a warm moon
and warm air floating under your clothes
and through your hair.
Then you'd think of heaven
where there's peace, away from here
and you'd go some place unreal
where everybody goes after something happens,
set up in the air, safe, a room in a hotel.
A brass bed, military hair brushes,
a couple of coats, trousers, maybe a dress
on a chair or draped on the floor.
This room is not on earth, feel the air,
warm like heaven and far away.

This is a place
where marriage nights are kept
and sometimes here you say, Hello
to a neat girl with you
and sometimes she laughs
because she thinks it's funny to be sitting here
for no reason at all, except perhaps,
she likes you daddy.

Maybe this isn't heaven but near
to something like it,
more like love coming up in elevators
and nothing to think about, except, O God,
you love her now and it makes no difference
if it isn't spring. All seasons are warm
in the warm air
and the brass bed is always there.

If you've done something
and the cops get you afterwards, you
can't remember the place again,
away from cops and streets—
it's all unreal—
the warm air, a dream
that couldn't save you now.
No one would care
to hear about it,
it would be heaven
far away, dark and no music,
not even a girl there.

Dempsey, Dempsey

Everybody give the big boy a hand,
a big hand for the big boy, Dempsey,
failure king of the U.S.A.

Maybe the big boy's coming back,
there're a million boys that want to come back
with hell in their eyes and a terrible sock
that almost connects.
They've got to come back, out of the street,
out of some lowdown, lousy job
or take the count with Dempsey.

When he's on his knees for the count
and a million dollars cold,
a million boys go down with him
yelling:
       Hit him again Dempsey,
kill him for me Dempsey,
Christ' sake Dempsey,
my God they're killing Dempsey,
It's Dempsey down, Dempsey, Dempsey.

The million men and a million boys,
come out of hell and crawling back,
maybe they don't know what they're saying,
maybe they don't dare,
but they know what they mean:
knock down the big boss,
O, my little Dempsey,
my beautiful Dempsey
with that Godinheaven smile

and quick, god's body leaping,
not afraid, leaping, rising—
hit him again, he cut my pay check, Dempsey.
My God, Dempsey's down—
he cut my pay check—
Dempsey's down, down,
the bastards are killing Dempsey.
Listen, they made me go to war
and somebody did something wrong to my wife
while I was gone.
Hit him again Dempsey, don't be a quitter
like I am Dempsey,
O, for Jesus Christ, I'm out.
I can't get up, I'm dead, my legs
are dead, see, I'm no good,
down for the count.
They got me and I'm out,
I've quit, quit again,
only God save Dempsey, make him get up again,
Dempsey, Dempsey.

A Boy of Twenty

Sometimes I hear my name
come up the stairs and walk
through noises in the hall . . .
but sounds all seem the same
in here, alone at night:
every sound that's made
seems to answer back
until I feel afraid
that chairs and tables talk
at me and want to walk
like noises in the hall
and slide along the wall.

My mouth feels large and black—
I want to answer back
at them.
        My lips are tight,
tight shut.
        Alone at night,
I sometimes think and feel
some thing of steam and steel
goes crazy and it's falling
in broken, crazy poses,
half-killed . . .
          and sick and crawling,
falls down on tangled streets,
(streets that the dark sky closes
at both ends, then it meets
itself again, up far
with half a moon and star . . .
above the tangled streets,

above the sounds that call
up stairways in the hall.)

I never answer back
to sounds that seem the same
as those that make my name,
for noises in the hall
are not my name at all . . .

The Sailor

An albatross goes flapping high:
he's a shadow in the sky,
far away and far astern,
following and following
like a song you used to sing
but you can't remember how
all the words went, nor the turn
of the melody and now
only half a tune and rhyme
circles in your head and yet
it's a thing you can't forget—
following you all the time.

An albatross is like a girl
you go picking up at night
in the street . . . or anywhere,
and she'll let you muss her hair
till you get it out of curl—
then she'll kiss you, more or less,
even let you tear her dress. . . .
but she's always far away,
far and almost out of sight. . . .
always like that goddam bird,
like the song you used to sing
that you wish you never heard. . . .
following and following,
all astern of men and ships
following.

9

And what I say
tastes like bilge against my lips. . . .

Boy, when a man dies, shipmates toss
his body to the albatross.

Hagen

Hagen is dead.
His girl remembers
his quick, bright head,
his well-washed hands
and his lean fingers
and how his cough stained
her bedroom floor.

He'd cough the moon
and a gallon of stars
red as fire torn
from a hundred wars.

All that could cure him
was "faith, hope and charity"—
she couldn't pay his
doctor bills
(and he wouldn't take pity
from her, nor tears).
There'd be no money
in the wills
he'd leave if he lived
a thousand years.

Hagen is dead.
All you can do with him
is dig up his coffin and
look at him there:
he wouldn't be changed much—
he looked like that anyway
and he'd still have

neat, red hair
and a quick, bright head.
That's all you can do.
Hagen is dead.

Rachel

He's a good Jewish boy,
why does he keep
telling how rotten things
grow in his sleep . . .
come in his sleep
and fall into his eyes:
dead men and crazy girls
walking through houses and
into the street,
dead men and crazy girls
selling red flowers for
pieces of meat.
Doesn't he know that they're
nothing but lies,
lies that he makes in his
head when he says
I am his mother and
he is my father and
King God will marry us
in a white dress
from his beard to his feet,
with no shoes on his feet,
standing on air
while we sit on the floor,
kissing and kissing and . . .

I am afraid of him;
I wish I didn't
love him anymore.

O Metaphysical Head

The man was forever haunted by his head,
this John Brown's body head—
John Brown's body lies—
John Brown's body lies—
John Brown's body lies—
Its head goes marching on—
triumphant, bowing to its friends,
lost in a crowd, then bright as dawn
found again, shining through streets,
laughing, happy by god, drunk, merry old head,
two cocktails and a bottle of champagne
lighting the dark corners in its brain.

A taxi. Home. O metaphysical head,
the world is too small for it,
barefooted, naked in a bedroom. Bed.
It is awake, remembering, thinking:
(I have seen this head too often,
this too-familiar head, yet it changes, changes. . . .
I have seen this young Caesar head
rising above a summer hill, bland and omnipotent,
to meet its love, to see her rise
to this head and with closing eyes
and open lips drinking
the head down until
its brain enters her body
and its will
becomes her will.)
And now, the head goes rolling down the hill,
(uxorious head)
rolls into darkness, sleeps:

grows large in dreams, serene, awful,
becomes God, opens its mighty lips
crying, Let there be light
in this dream. Let
all the women who have not worshipped
this head come naked and ashamed before it,
suffering their little children
to come unto it.
Pity for little children,
conceived in sin,
not fathered by this head
but from the needs
of other men.

Awake again, rising from the dream
into the bedroom, eyelids closed,
the head lost in space,
fixed in ecstatic peace,
senses warm, fluid in the body,
but the head, the winged, haloed head gone,
gone where all godheads go,
singing, Heaven, heaven . . .
                              No,
found somewhere in a gutter,
pitiful, blind, sallow.
(And curious friends examine it,
saying, It shall never rise again,
poor fellow,
put it away.
It hurts us.
Poor fellow,
no words were made to say
how sad we feel. An ugly head—
see what's become of John—
we're sorry, but we must be moving on.)

The head gone. Irrevocably gone,
no longer magnificent, the speaker of the word,
divine, exalted, tilting backward in a barber's chair,
august, revered,
floating above a glass-topped desk,
making its power heard
roaring into a telephone,
then brisk, attentive,
meeting its clients and its creditors,
then finally tired, meditating restfully
on the flat bosoms of its stenographers,
on the undetermined virginity of its stenographers.

There would be no offices for headless men,
no girls, nor wives,
only the subway entrances where one may stand
unseeing (almost unseen)
with right arm raised, the index finger of the hand
pointing where the head had been,
the left hand catching pennies.
John Brown's body goes
begging underground,
John Brown's body—
(No one would dare look at the creature;
it could stand,
a monument for years,
headless, quiet,
forever catching pennies
in its hand.)

McAlpin Garfinkel, Poet

It is enough for me to tremble,
my vital organs directed toward the sun,
toward the stars,
trembling.

It is better for me to stand at street corners
staring at women, seeing their bodies flowering
like new continents, hills warm in sunshine and
long deep rivers,
(even as I am,
trembling)
than to be nothing, to fade away in grass and stone.

It is better for me to believe nothing
than to be nothing,
better for me
not to fight, to let cops and truck drivers
crash through my brains, trample my entrails,
O let me cry out my rage against millions,
carry my remains to the President,
up the steps of the White House
to be deodorized by the Department of Justice
and the Secretary of State,
thenceforth expunged
from the Congressional Record.
(But I shall be intact,
no word spoken,
like laughter in my mother's womb, a pointless joke
with no beginning and no end)
And if you hear me crying: My God, my God, my God

down streets and alleys,
I am merely trembling (afraid, my God, my God,
to be nothing, to fade away
in grass, in stone.)

Time and Isidore Lefkowitz

It is not good to feel old
for time is heavy,
time is heavy
on a man's brain,
thrusting him down,
gasping into the earth,
out of the way of the sun
and the rain.

Look at Isidore Lefkowitz,
biting his nails, telling how
he seduces Beautiful French Canadian
Five and Ten Cent Store Girls,
beautiful, by God, and how they cry
and moan, wrapping their arms
and legs around him
when he leaves them
saying:
Good bye,
good bye.

He feels old when he tells
these stories over and over,
(how the Beautiful Five and Ten Cent Store
Girls go crazy when he puts on
his clothes and is gone),
these old lies
that maybe nobody at all believes.
He feels old thinking how
once he gave five
dollars to a girl

who made him feel like other men
and wonders if she is still alive.
If he were a millionaire,
if he could spend five dollars now,
he could show them how
he was strong and handsome then,
better than other men.

But it is not good to feel old,
time is too heavy,
its gets a man
tired, tired
when he thinks how time wears
him down
and girls, milk-fed, white,
vanish with glorious smiling millionaires
in silver limousines.

Advice

You can't fight God,
I know the facts, I said
to Mabel: I know what's going to happen,
it always does. You might as well be dead
if you get violent, he gets you.
I've seen him work before,
I said to her:
You wake up at night violent—
you wish to Christ the Woolworth Tower were
ten thousand stories high
and you on top nude naked, shouting at God,
shouting, 'Get out of my sky.
It's mine. I went the limit with Jake—
it's my affair.
I don't know where he's gone, or if he's dead,
or if he goes
to hell.'

'I'm going to jump. I'm going to make a splash
and spoil somebody's nice clean suit of clothes.
This sky is mine.
I got a right to jump.
I'm tired of my eyes and hair,
my arms and legs, I've seen them all
since I was born.
They're going to fall
in one grand smash. I got a right
to tell my boss to go to hell this way
and get some other fool to take my job
and wait a week for Saturday'.

21

I said, 'God's watching you:
they'll call the wagon then,
they'll run you into Bellevue,
fighting like tigers in a crazy zoo
to get you into bed and hold you there
with a strong arm doctor feeling you to see
what's wrong and ask you where
Jake is and calm you down.
And the screams
of crazy women in the halls
will be like whispers in your dreams.
They'll make you go to sleep in sleep that seems
like sleep forever'.

'And when they let you out
you'll be quiet, you won't try
to take a drink of lysol for they might
get you again. Until you die
you'll keep yourself a secret,
talking to yourself in the streets,
fighting God on Broadway.
I know how God works,' I told her,
'when you fight his laws.'
I saw what was going to happen

and it always does.

Bridgewater Jones: Impromptu in a Speakeasy

When you've been through what I've been through
over in France where war was hell
and everything turned to blood and mud
and you get covered with blood and rain
and rain and mud
then you come back home again,
come back home and make good in business.
You don't know how and you don't know why;
it's enough to make God stand still and wonder.
It's something that makes you sit down and think
and you want to say something that's clear and deep,
something that someone can understand:
that's why I got to be confidential
and see things clear and say what I mean,
something that's almost like a sermon,
O world without end,
amen.

When you can't see things then you get like Nelly
and somebody has to put you out
and somebody has to put you away
but you can always see through Nelly.
She unrolled like a map on the office floor,
you could see her in the dark—
a blind pink cat
in the back seat of the Judge's car.
But she'd get cold in the Globe Hotel,
singing songs like the Songs of Solomon,
making the Good Book sound immoral
then she'd say she was Mother Mary
and the strength of sin is the law.

World without end
amen.

Gentlemen, I had to fire Nelly,
she didn't see when a man's in business,
she didn't know when a man's a Christian
you can't go singing the Songs of Solomon,
shouting Holy, holy, holy,
making Mother of Christ a whore,
cold as rain,
dead blood and rain like the goddam war,
cold as Nelly telling you hell you killed her baby,
then she couldn't take a letter
but would sit down and cry
like rain.

It got so bad I couldn't sleep
with her hair and eyes and breasts and belly
and arms around me
like rain, rain,
rain without end
amen.

I tell you gentlemen almighty God,
I didn't kill her dead baby,
it was the rain
falling on men and girls and cities.
Ask the Judge (he's got a girl)
about a baby:
a baby wants life and sun, not rain by God that's death
            when you float a baby down the sewer into the
                            East River with its lips
making foam at the stern of ships
head on for Liverpool in rain.

You can't see what happens in rain
(only God knows, world without end)
maybe war, maybe a dead baby.
There's no good when rain falls on a man;
I had to make it clear,
that's what I wanted to explain.

The Medium

Spirits rousing out of air—
they are here and shut between
gasps of time that dead men share
with the graveyard and the bell
that swings their bones with music down . . .
and down . . . down . . .
where cold Caesar fell
open eyed.
      I knew a man
who fed his wits on such as these
to guard himself from tall, dark streets
where women's flesh grew white and trees
were frozen in an iron square . . .

And on him came a caravan
of noises that went through his veins . . .

He smiled at ghosts, then took a bride
from old, green Egypt, for her breath
filled his lungs with ancient prayer,
till, he too, closed his lips and died.

Love Song: Twenty-Third Street

There was a pale gold girl coming out of Asia,
walking out of Asia with white hills behind her,
out of the deep noise of Buddha and Jehovah,
she came walking where swift waves stir.

There were drunken bells in great temples of thunder,
ringing out full prayers to sad priests in the sunshine,
heavy with black cloth and senile with hunger,
they drank impotence in red wine.

Away she came then, but always out of Asia;
she is always walking from out of the sorrow,
from the curved loins of the black god, Jehovah,
rising behind her where dark winds blow.

Dilemma on Twenty-Third Street

Why should I leave him;
he's good to me.
God, but he's beautiful
with ice-gold hair:
look at his eyes now—
blue from the sea,
cut by the wind
to a short, bright stare.

He says I can't go—
can't leave his blood
that runs through my thighs and
I can't walk away . . .
He gives me power
to move as I should
and all too soon
I'll be still someday.

He stands above me
and over my head
just as the trees rise
out of the ground
into wet clouds
that mingle and spread
falling in rain and
in one deep sound.

Maybe my legs won't
walk: hip and knee,
feet are his mind
with his thoughts inside.

why should I leave him;
he's good to me . . .

Maybe the world
isn't new and wide.

Prisoner's Song

O, Mary's lovelier than anything that grows
out of spring trees that stir
April when my mind goes
around and over her.

I love her more than skies bright with the wind and sun
and all my thoughts arise
to travel, one by one,
into her lips and eyes.

She shuts me in her; she holds all my blood and brain
under her lock and key.
Christ! I'm in jail again—
she'll never let me free.

Sometimes, my blind dreams float far—like a wanderer
I go away, remote;
then I return to her
with panic in my throat.

No Cock Crows at Morning

There is no cock crowing in our bedroom,
waking good morning startled by his cries:
the great bird has vanished in a fiery dream,
his clamorous wings are shut
and his rolling golden eye
has gone blind
and his radiant comb is a laurel of ashes.

Listen, there is no cock crowing
(Somebody murdered someone else's wife
and left a pool of blood in the subway,
crying his matins out of gothic type,
shouting the resurrection and the life,
rising in vapors from an invisible flame,
sloughing his shirt and trousers
in an electric chair)

There is no cock crowing,
but there is a phantom bird walking
through prison walls, walking through streets and houses
silent, invulnerable, walking over the dead—
over the martyrs and the wrongdoers
there is no cock crowing.

Unfriendly Discourse

I

What do you want for your money?
Sleep,
only more sleep,
trying to remember to forget
somewhere in sleep a dog barks
out of darkness like the roar
of guns following you forever
in war
sunk in your blood.

To remember to forget
a million miles of stone
over your head, under your feet.
Remember to forget but hold
these things somewhere in your brain a minute,
victory a minute:

Eddie Kowolski, lightweight champion,
steel body like a piston
shot through air
gets his man,
gets him down
                 buries him into the canvas,
pounds him soft, rivets him
into the earth.

Victory a minute, that's all,
darkness again.
The crowd yells:

32

We want another victory,
victory, by God, victory!
Remember only to forget but hold
another victory:

John Bayliss, bigamist, bookkeeper,
kills his wife,
looks into her body, his eyes X ray machines
counting her bones
                              (sees all,
will tell all later)
victory now,
something done, finished now
(grief and sobs later)

The crowd yells:
                              victory,
we want more victory,
after long jobs, after long nights at home,
victory!

2

These things remember and remembering,
forget again
like the sun thrown flat against buildings
at evening
                 perishing in grandeur:
There are a million beautiful girls
born yesterday, maybe a week ago,
maybe back a thousand years,
saying,

"Once I was beautiful in Embryo, Tennessee,
look at me now

33

and take me back to Embryo,
here is no place to be
beautiful;
            legs and arms
are shadows.
                  They are real only
at home
        in Embryo,
take me away."

The grounds sinks, the brain flounders,
drinking down
years of darkness,
forgetting to remember the sun,
only hell for your money,
remembering.

Hellbabies

Hellbabies sitting in speakeasies
trying to make a million dollars come to life
out of a shot of gin,
trying to make love again
to a new girl,
trying to get out of the way
of sleep and death.

Hellbabies (another brood)
walking through rain,
electric signboards,
in subways,
at shop windows,
their brains filled with tears,
trying to get out of the way
of wives and children
because there are
     NO JOBS, NO JOBS
no work, only walking.

Maybe God is waiting for
these hellbabies,
surely, hell is waiting
for them to come home:

come home, there will be sweet hell tonight,
always ready.

The Young Wife

I left my job on my wedding day
   (sleep, my pussy cat, sleep, sleep, sleep)
where walls and skies were brown and gray
I worked ten years on sweat-shop pay;
I'd earn my clothes when the boss felt gay
   (sleep, sleep, sleep)

And all my husband doesn't know
   (sleep, my pussy cat, sleep, sleep, sleep)
is good for him. And I can go
back to my boss. He wants me—though
I'm not for trusting men, high or low,
   (sleep sleep sleep)

I wait for evening all day through
   (sleep, my pussy cat, sleep, sleep, sleep)
no supper's made. A meal or two
a man forgets while love is new—
and he'll forgive me as all men do
   (sleep sleep sleep)

Interior: The Suburbs

There is no rest for the mind
in a small house. It moves, looking for God
with a mysterious eye fixed on the bed,
into a cracked egg at breakfast,
looking for glory in an arm chair,
or simply noting the facts of life
in a fly asleep upon the ceiling.
The mind, sunk in quiet places,
(like old heroes) sleeps no more
but walks abroad in a slouch hat,
quick with adultery at violent street corners,
then trembling, returns,
sadly directs its mysterious eye
into a coffee cup—there is no rest—
for there are many miles to walk in the small house,
traveling past the same chairs, the same tables,
the same glassy portraits on the walls,
flowing into darkness.

There is no victory in the mind
but desperate valor
shattering the four walls,
disintegrating human love
until the iron-lidded mysterious eye
(lowered carefully with the frail body
under churchyard gardens)
stares upward, luminous, inevitable,
piercing solar magnitudes
on a fine morning.

Homestead

This house rises into a metallic sky
a brilliant iron lake under its porticos,
under its balconies and watch towers multiplied
beyond reason and (one, two, three, four) exact calculation.
An institution for the blind,
a sailors' rest (home from the seas)
not quite, but the specific hiding place where John
McCumber Bluethorn, millionaire, sleeps (falls asleep)
after a dozen cocktails.
                    Expects to die
in the inevitable stronghold for his nerves and tissues.
The bright machinery that was his mind
falls silent.
                 His factories (men in the street
crying against him and the quick rifles of the State Militia
are quiet now)
                  Here is the last retreat.
The legend of his wives, his children safe,
locked in iron waters.
                        His mind, fallen inward, stirs no more,
only the house rises;
count the bricks, the stones
and estimate their power
against wind and rain, time and dissolution.

O Mors Aeterna

Be for a little while eternal,
singing with all the songs in your body
but making no sound.

The Rose of Sharon singing in an old city
was eternal suddenly
for a little while.

And the mountains fell away
and the city sank into earth again
and the voices of dead men came from the ground
crying incest and poverty and murder
(all in the many dead years
that had sent them into the earth)
but now rising, crying against the world
and mortal sun and moon and stars,
against loss and the masters
in purple victories, clothed with iron wars.

For a little while
the Rose of Sharon sang eternally
until the city came round her again
and there was no sound.

NO RETREAT

(1933)

FOR PATRICK AND JOANNA

Stanzas for My Daughter

Tell her I love
                she will remember me
always, for she
is of love's graces made;
                      she will remember
these streets where the moon's shade
falls and my shadow mingles
with shadows sprung
from a midnight tree.

Tell her I love that I
am neither in earth nor sky,
stone nor cloud,
but only this
walled garden she knows well
and which her body is.

Her eyes alone shall make
me blossom for her sake;
contained within her, all
my days shall flower or die,
birthday or funeral
concealed where no man's eye
finds me unless she says:
He is my flesh and I
am what he was.

Live beyond hope,
                beyond October trees
spent with fire, these
ministers of false Spring
                      making our bodies stir

with spurious flowering
under snow that covers
hope and hopeful lovers
and fades in timeless seas.

Live beyond hope, my care
that makes a prison for your eyes (and hair
golden as autumn grass
swept by the morning sun)
for you shall walk with praise
when all my ways are run.

Take all my love, but spend
such love to build your mind
against hope that leaves behind
my winter night and snow
falling at the year's end.

Tell her I know
               that living is too long
for our love to endure;
the tenuous and strong
web of time (outlasting
girls and men—love's rapid signature
of hand and lip and eye)
gleams as if wires were strung
across a sunset sky.

Tell her that girls and men
are shadows on the grass
where time's four seasons pass;
tell her that I have seen
               O many a nervous queen
of girls (Madonna, glorious
white-towered goddess) fade

while walking in noon's shade,
separate limbs and foreheads bright,
now dim, anonymous. . . .

Tell her I love
                to make these words a song
with her careful lips,
                O bride,
Spring and bridegroom at your side,
save them for the deep and long
silences when northstar light
perishes down quicksilver steep
walls of flesh where love and death
make a counterfeit of sleep.

Take this wreath to celebrate
union of the fire and rain,
bone and tissue.
                Sleep, O bride,
for the waking limbs divide
into separate walls again.

Tell her that flesh is spirited
into earth:
                this wreath is grown
from black bronze roots to weave a crown
for the death mask and the head
fixed with its metallic smile
upward where generations climb
making garlands of their own
out of iron and of stone.

Birthday in April

This is the day that I began; this is New Year's
in the terse calendar that opens with my name.
April and south winds in the sky repeat the same
rhythm and the identical body sleeps, hears
Spring at morning waking the same trees that always
wear the sun on slender branches that somehow rise
out of dark streets curved downward at night and men's eyes
cannot discern the roots coiled and unwinding under
doors and hallways.

It is not the season but inevitable
return of seasons that destroys the days, the hours
fixed in a man's brain and builds them new again: flowers
and grass covering a ruined city. And full
of these quick seasons, I retrace the day my breath
first issued toward my third decade. Let stones, spires, earth,
O Trinity, answer death.

Tombstone with Cherubim

No notice in the papers:
                              a cold voice over the telephone
saying she was dead.
                              Somebody whispered, "Syphilis,"
a sentimental lie.
                              Somebody said,
"She was rococo, a Florentine olive tree
cut down and stripped beneath the body
of a football-captain-stock-broker asleep
upon Miami sands."
                              "She shrieked at poverty.
Divorced from silk, furs, and patented nickel-plated
limousines."
                              She loved unsought, relaxed security
drifting to bed with men as though they were
exotic dreams.
                              "Damn Marie,
you should have gone out like a row of mazda lamps
smashed with a crowbar."
                              These were the legends.

The facts are these:
(true enough for a beautiful girl
who held a glimpse of midnight in her hair)
I saw her pacing with unforgettable ease
down Michigan Boulevard one autumn morning.

                              She died in Lesbian serenity
neither hot nor cold
                              until the chaste limbs stiffened.
Disconnect the telephone. Cut the wires.

A Wreath for Margery

Telegrams, letters, voices: what did we hear?
They whispered, *Death*.
               And her last word
was *Love* ... She might have said,

Cover my body with quick grass—
I'll live beyond
self, husband, childbirth, death
into fair earth—look how my fiery hair
falls into ashes.
             Flames fall to whiteness,
and in her curtained room pale candles glow:
new linen veils the eyes that now see only
winter's twilight and voyages of snow.

Then let her body rest: the body's spirit
wakes through widening eyes
bucolic blue Wisconsin summer skies,
and from her throat the music small birds sing,
as fine, as rare
as the swift glinting radiance of her hair
glimpsed at within a glass, the window where
daylight spends its last fires against the wall.

2

And there were pastoral places that knew her well,
that saw her dressed as if her favorite season
were far from home, that saw her turn away
farewells unspoken,
only the shadow of her disappearing smile:

48

Portage, Wisconsin birth-place, the slow mile
of dark catalpas, and the river inland
to Mississippi waters, the far ocean
southward, then green-wave-leaping
Caribbean Sea . . .

In pastoral quiet, hear the deeper silence
broken and in the dark that magnifies
white cattle plunging homeward, fasten bars
to guard receding meadows against the night:
the corn leans towards the pale north star
and fructifies its light.
So this fertility of earth restores
our union with the white tides of the moon
within our blood and we
who share the restless earth's vitality
turn away forever from our inland shores . . .

  Only in sleep may we again discover
  the lost, the waiting seasons under snow,
  roots of another year,
  the harvest reaped and scattered—

and is this secret way too deep, too far
to climb the calendar
toward summer mornings and the golden-glow
sumach and sunflower? . . .
we wake in foreign lands and find diminished
our lonely sloping valleys and green plains.

3

We who have walked through city streets recall—
(Try to remember sunlight in a glass!)—
full-blossomed girls out of old histories
had ways like hers: their breath

in small Greek flowers—
see how their hands plead with us, reach through darkness—
suddenly her shadow meets me at the door
then turns to guide me up a waiting stair.
This was her room: the same, whatever address:
New York, Chicago, Portage, Santa Fe.

Windows hinge open: see
swept floors, cleared table, neat chintz chair—
the room vaults into space, revolves in air.

    The luminous image fades, yet wanders near.

Her limbs are rivers flowing past the town—
in plangent waters where catalpas drown.

Sunday Morning News: The Picture Section

And did you see the face:
the wide Augustan eye
that pierces stellar space?
Gaze deeply on this face
whose features never die
but are restored again
from bronze and curried stone,
nostril and broad cheek bone
carved out of memory,
his face like other men's
where shrewd mortality
uncovers them again
engraved in bronze, in stone.

    Put Charles the Bald in that corner of the museum:
    the brain so light, the limbs so heavy
    no horse could carry him;
    and over there, Napoleon's son
    whose eyes held midnight in two spheres,
    the two lost kingdoms his.

Hail him inheritor
of millions—
                Was it men
or stocks or acres or . . . ?
Count all his wealth again.

    Intangibles of power are written in ticker tape
    on private yachts: ring them up on the cash register,
    cable them from Maine to Singapore
    around the world tonight.

Remark the stallion eye
the white-lipped masonry.
The mouth endures beyond
brass written monuments
where sleepless deserts lie.
And did you hear the name?
Each with a different name
but the anatomy,
limbs, torso quite the same;
the head abrupt, secure,
the face looks toward the sky.

Praise to John Skelton

Praise to John Skelton and
his naked, sinewy rhyme:
the frosty bitten seed
furrowed from his right hand—
root, trunk and branches speed
to flower in our time.

John Skelton, laureate,
doctor divinity,
stripped grandeur from the great
who towered in simony—
uncloaked the cardinal
and Wolsey's skeleton
sloughed lace and crook and pall,
thighbone and carrion,
meet for the carousel!

Skull and charred ribs disclose
how the worm eats the rose,
how the worm, jew'led and fat,
sits with a mitred hat,
eats at the king's right side:
sing loud Magnificat!

John Skelton, laureate,
whose sun has risen late
never to close its eye
in our eternity,
opened the lips that preach
virtue in English speech,
the ragged adder's tongue,

sharp, deep and venomous
iron and mirth,
then tart and ruddy song
heard when spring's morning wakes
April whose blossom shakes
birds over earth.

Here is no epitaph—
wreathed coffin, yew and hearse,
poet, to sink your verse
in burial again:
for these lines celebrate
your quick, immortal state:
body, hands, lips and eyes
speak metered gold.

Amen

And of Columbus

Columbus is remembered by young men
who walk the world at night in street-walled prisons:
Where is my country? Why do I return
at midnight to a moonlit, inland ocean
whose waves beat as a heart beats in my side?

Is the return to these receding shores
the end of earth, fallen to deep-sea traffic,
the end of all things?

The cities that coil upward
from sumac bush and sand flow into grass:
roofs, towers mingle
with roots and the bodies of men who died
in foreign wars.

> Columbus who believed his own miracles,
conquered his India, oceans, mermaids, golden savages—
where was his country?

> It was a small stone room at night
in darkness. And time echoes time saying: Columbus no more,
where stars move toward the sun.

And in Havana under the Southern Cross, all that is his
is where his bones lie.

Emerson: Last Days at Concord

Enter America at Concord's bridge,
true marriage of the east and west, Brahma
whose lips nurse at my veins.
                              Where was the green brass cannon
sunken in churchyards after the shots were fired?
Listen, the world is sleeping and the noise
coils in thunder where Dover's beach
shall wake no more
                    and the Indian ocean
pours its blood into the sun when evening's tide
uncovers bones upon the shore.
                              Cut me a frock coat, for the oversoul
lies naked: parts, limbs exposed
within a broken coffin. O light that stirs in dust
as eastwind darkens nightfall into rain.
                              Where are your lips, hands,
  Brahma?
What was the name, your name or mine?

                              Come, friend,
we shall walk in the west orchard drinking russet wine,
kiss daisies where the transcendental tree
(look how the death worm feeds upon its roots)
shelters our love and fiery blossoms fall in Plato's vineyard.
I have carried the world in my brain, have seen its heroes
diminish,
            saw oceans, continents dissolve in sunlight
on Concord window sills:
                              Are you my friend?
Then here's my secret; I have forgotten
all friends and the words that joined my lips to theirs.

Better to keep faith
                    and believe
no one. Better to be a patriot disowning
this land. Give back America to sunlight, wind and rain;
set sail for India from Concord's bridge,
leap to the quarter-deck where our Columbus
once more commands his ships.
                              Is that a storm in the sky?
And are these apples ripe? I grew this orchard to be a paradise
this side of Eden.

Salvos for Randolph Bourne

O Bitterness never spoken, the death mask etched in silver,
the dark limbs rolled in lead where the shallow grave conceals
despair: the image of a large head, forward, devouring
the collarbone. No general in brass over it and no
conquering angel kneels.

This was the end:
                    There were no firing squads,
no City Hall Nathan Hale with a bronze cord at his throat
                       speaking of lives and his country
                          (where the generations came,
rose, wavered, scattered like a great sea coiling
against rock-buttressed walls that disappear
into a shoreline of weeds and sand.)

Only a small room and a million words to be written before mid-
    night
against poverty and idiot death like the gray face of Emerson
fading in New England winter twilight; the hard face vanishing
in snow, the passionately soft words issuing from the mouth.
Listen to the rock, the oracle no longer there!

To be the last American, an embryo coiled in a test tube,
to be a fixed and paralytic smile cocked upward to the clouds,
to see friends and enemies depart (around the corner)
their sticks and smart fedoras bright in sunlight,
to be or not to be Hamlet, the Prince of Wales,
or last week's New Republic;
to be death delicately walking between chimney pots on Eighth
    Street,
possibly this is best to be
                      or not to be.

CHORUS
FOR SURVIVAL

(1935)

FOR BRYHER

One

Tell us that love
                returns,
O Hymen, sing
In every hour that burns
After the midnight hour
In darkness here.
                Wake with thy song
The antique smiling year,
Always thy axis turning to restore
The Greek dawn breaking
On Aegean seas.
                Break here
The silent wave upon the shore
In dreams to darkness-driven memories;
Wake with thy song,
Tell us to wake and sing—
Midnight and starlight night are always long
For the impatient young.
Open gray skies and fling
Thy yellow veil, the sun,
                      down city streets
Where tireless seasons run,
Speed here October, our retarded spring,
Daylight and green
Live forests blossoming:
The wave-washed rock in embers glowing red,
Wake even here,
                till climbing overhead,
Window and cornice on steel branches bear
Fire of morning from another spring.

Wake with thy song
                    time-darkened waters
That have not reached their end
Westward to India, passage through storm,
Bearing the image of a Grecian bride,
Eyes like cornflowers staring at our side,
The blue flame lighting darkness in the shade
Of trees knee-deep in grass
At summer's tide....
Again our lips recall
That she was beautiful:
                        the pure
Alcestis memory of a kiss,
                          the violet-
Scented breast, the virginal
Breathing light in sunlit air;
Handclasp remembers hand,
                          quick limbs enthrall
Entwining limbs, the nervous, flexible
Growing green grapevine,
                        until the blood
Flows into sleep and blood is wine.

This is thy memory, America,
The tenuous marriage of disunited blood
Captain and slave one bed,
                          in dust until the wind
Stirs dust to life again ...
                          and walking here,
Conquered and conqueror
(The apple blossoms white in midnight hair).

Wake with thy song
Even in death (they sleep like death)
Men in the wilderness

(The night is long)
                        breaking through forests of a foreign land,
Sell and move on.
Westward we follow to an unknown star
And shall not come again the way we came.

Tell us that love
               returns
After the midnight hour
In darkness here,

Season of iron cities against the sky,
The cold room where I write my signature
Toward my survival in the waning year:
Winter and frost, each day revolves to night,
The longer night that brings a short tomorrow
Of middle age in dark, divided faces,
In faces that I know too well, my own
Face staring likeness in the mirror
Beyond the hour of death or hope or doom;
When doors swing wide upon an empty room,
Window and door open to empty air
Echo in darkness of the lost frontier.

Wake with thy song
               the voices
Of men who cannot sleep:
                      We count our losses
In decimals of time, the ten per cent
Of what we hope: To let:
                     the naked bed, the folding chair,
Space for the body motionless in air,
Permit survival if we stand alone.
Voiceless we smile; we are not violent.

63

And from these places
On the abyss of loss,
                              the steel-edged towers
Pierce the moon, the sun:
Look where Atlantis leaves forgotten traces,
Empire of empty houses under seas.

This is thy heritage, America,
Scaffold of iron deep in stone.
                              Destroy the ruins,
This is the place; wreck here and build again.

Tell us that love
                    returns,
Not soft nor kind,
But like a crystal turning in the mind,
Light where the body is:
                              thy limbs are fire
Walking alive among the ancient trees,
The ruined town, cathedral wall, church spire.

Say love, through always young,
Remembers these . . .
                         place, house we entered
And shall not return . . .
                              Spirit that outlives time
To join our hands in love,
                              do you remember
Serpent and dove, the wild rose and the thorn,
Blossom and leaf in secret flowering
Read in a book of broken prophecies?

Wake with thy song
                         (I speak a difficult and treacherous tongue
That was not made for wedding song or carol;

Measure my dwindling shadow on the wall,
Wait for the silence when my lips are gone
That say:
              Though night is long, this bitter hour wakes
And is not sterile).

Wake here
              Atlantis under hard blue skies,
Thy Indian Summer bride is like the spring
Roof-tree in light
                      thy blossoming
In fire to love returns.

Two

Down traffic signals on Park Avenue,
down chromium light imperfect past revealed
in a museum, heart of reality within a dream,
enter New York,
                    the city in a mirror
of Rome, and the calm faces like our own,
even the cracked cheekbone and hollowed eye,
the look of power and sadness and disunion:

   And they were clever
   as we are clever now, eating their heart
   until the breast rang hollow and the remains
   were set on end, secure:
   Hail Caesar, God, erect, the man in stone.
   There in the circus where they stared: the terror:
   the cry for bread
                       and dark sky closed above them.
Apollo's fluid arm embracing shadows
of Asia fallen by Scamander's side,
Athens, the urn, Greek bride of quietness,
descending,
                 turn to see the quickened head
fading in dust . . . the silent legion tread
in tremulous air at Riverside, Grant's Tomb.

The Muse grows old, her lips a quarter-smile
toward death in ruins: there, the black stallion
the horse of poetry, black over white,
the dance in quietness, museum twilight
theirs, forever falling. . .

Through windows east, the city leans, brick, steel,
deep-banked and floating Chinese Wall looms over
dockyard and river tenement, the poor.

Mirror the city of electric star
light into light
                    on sleepless, quiet faces
less real than statues of the thing they were,
the open hand upon each empty breast.

New York closed into Rome, Rome into Egypt,
Cosmopolis, and only darkness there.

Three

Waking from sleep we heard the Great Lakes' tide,
clear spray in wind, white blossoming in dark
night bloom, the city's heat behind us, rolling back
miles westward over plains.
                                    Only the sound
of tide, the water leaping these shores,
the lake in wind and in trees over us, the voices
rising in spray, the white tide breaking.
Came Pere Marquette down rivers to the sea,
the inland ocean, bright in wilderness,
sumac and pine.

"Earn heaven for this earth, and iron-blue sky,
the fire-green leaf in the stilled waters—
water, air, fire in my hand, my veins these rivers
flowing to the cross whose flower is man;
the holy tree, blood-red with fruit, the resurrection
waking in this land.
Spring here God's arch, and choir singing praise
through pine and maple crucifix—
                                    the forest
trembling with light: O fiery bough."
                                    The Eucharist in snow,
death's supper underground and the long winter
under foreign stars.

Four

Ask no return for love that's given
embracing mistress, wife or friend,
                              ask no return:
on this deep earth or in pale heaven,
awake and spend
hands, lips, and eyes in love,
in darkness burn,
                    the limbs entwined until the soul ascend.

Ask no return of seasons gone:
the fire of autumn and the first hour of spring,
the short bough blossoming
through city windows when night's done,
when fears adjourn
                    backward in memory where all loves end

in self again, again the inward tree
growing against the heart
and no heart free.
From love that sleeps behind each eye
in double symmetry
                    ask no return,
even in enmity, look! I shall take your hand;
nor can our limbs disjoin in separate ways again,
walking, even at night on foreign land
through houses open to the wind, through cold and rain,
waking alive, meet, kiss and understand.

Five

Under the stone I saw them flow,
express Times Square at five o'clock,
eyes set in darkness, trampling down
all under, limbs and bodies driven
in crowds, crowds over crowds, the street
exit in starlight and dark air
to empty rooms, to empty arms,
wallpaper gardens flowering there,
error and loss upon the walls.

I saw each man who rode alone
prepare for sleep in deeper sleep
and there to ride, sightless, unknown,
to darkness that no day recalls.
Riderless home, shoulder to head,
feet on concrete and steel to ride
Times Square at morning and repeat
tomorrow's five o'clock in crowds
(red light and green for speed) descend,
break entrance home to love or hate
(I read the answer to the door)

the destination marked "Return,
no stop till here; this is the end."

Six

Through streets where crooked Wicklow flows
I saw a man with broken nose:
His venomous eyes turned full on me
And cursed the ancient poverty
That scarred his limbs and mired his clothes.

Beyond the street, beyond the town,
Rose hill and tree and sea and down:
O drear and shadowy green ash tree,
O hills that neither sleep nor rest
But are like waves in that dark sea
That rides the wind, nor'east, nor'west,

O cursed, wind-driven poverty!

Below the hill, below the town,
Deep, whispering voices everywhere
Break quiet in the morning air
And mount the skies to pierce the sun.

I saw the naked, cowering man
Shrink in the midnight of his eye,
There to eat bitterness within,
And close the door and hide the sin
That made his withering heart run dry.
O venomous, dark, unceasing eye
That turned on street and town and me,
Between the waves of hill and sea
Until his eyelid closed the sky.

   The rain-rilled, shaken, green ash tree
   Spread roots to gather him and me

In downward pull of earth that drains
The blood that empties through men's veins
Under the churchyard, under stone
Until the body lies alone
And will not wake: nor wind, nor sky
Bring sunlight into morning air
And breathe disquiet everywhere
Into the heart of hill and town.

O heart whose heart is like my own
And not to rest or sleep but climb
Wearily out of earth again
To feed again that venomous eye
That is the manhood of my time,
Whether at home or Wicklow town.
This is my street to walk again,
O cursed, wind-driven poverty,
                        I hear the coming of the rain.

Seven

"The voyage crossed, the firmament one star,
New found New England, home:
                              Now meet me there
In Concord's orchard where the apple bough
Swings over shoulder at the window pane
In the green season. . . .
                              Wake my limbs again
Adam-Ralph Emerson, the first man here;
Eden, the gate unlatched, this place my own.

*After a year's
travel Emerson
recrosses the
Atlantic and is
back home in
Concord, 1833*

And I have seen the world, heard the lark
    climbing
His golden sinuous music in dark air,
That speech unknown but to the subtlest ear
Echo through morning over St. Paul's dome,
Wing following through April's hemisphere,
Not less familiar now than earth at home:
England, the Colosseum of great minds.

*He recalls
London.*

Under deep trees, the bright-eyed mariner,
Coleridge, speaking and the music gone:
Miraculous white hair, the oracle
Voice descending, flowing on,

Knowing, perhaps, that I would understand:
Me, in a vision, under visionary eyes,
My pale, frail body and the profile spare,
Visible the wedding guest who must depart,
Must go like youth before the day is done,
Saying 'good-by' and clasp an aged hand.

73

Perhaps he knew, perhaps he saw....

Perhaps Carlyle

Read something in my veins.

We are a little mad

The Emersons, blood thin but deep and the quick
    body given

To God at bedtime, clipped within the spirit

In sleep, in prayers, the candle lit at dark

In homage to the sun.

Dissolve the body and the light is gone:

The stars expire and angels lose their glory,

The vertebrae within a nest of quiet

Between the sheets to fear the wind that stirs

Cypress and willow over us ...

Essential

I, the boy, the curious scientific dreaming eye

Fixed on the landscape ash tree, elm,

And rippling grass like water at low tide:

Trees' branches spars of Salem's ships that rode

Jewel-edged at sunset into Asia's side,

Her night our noon, her noonday our tomorrow,

The tropic desert silence under snow....

Lyceum

Lectures at the hearth at home, and in the fire
    there,

My boyhood saw

Greek islands floating over Harvard Square:

Homer, the blind head sleeping

In celestial seas;

Everett, the voice, asking whose lips were these

Come out of time to breathe our native air?

State House, the fallen stone Acropolis....

And at my hearth, the family Lyceum:

Feed the soul's sepulchre, they said, and hear

Dante the Florentine who walked to heaven,

74

Spiring in golden cages out of hell
To hail unearthly love, the Beatrice
Lady and bride,
                    spirit on the last hill
Of that high world,
                    O Paradiso!
And the last desire
Turned in a crystal image on the stair:
More beautiful than dress that angels wear
Was hers, whose waking limbs were cloaked with fire.

Read Thomas Gray, the graveyard nightingale,
The cold rhyme out of season, raven-dark
November-piercing death at April's core:
Love, fame, Cromwell or Milton sleep at last
In dust that circles at the cottage door. . . .
Worship and heresy: God's food, the devil's meat,
Black cloth and ashes where I sit to eat—

To be divine   *The rejection*
        (and through my heart great goodness flows) *of the ministry*
To walk in India at a Concord shrine.   *and Calvinism.*

        Bitter the thinking man who sees
        The careful millionaire, the red frontier
        In city walls closed; and the hot mills pour
        Iron for guns, starvation, war:
        To know too well, to think too long:

The bitter hours into seasons pass
Until the soul fills up,
Breaks, scatters backward into that better time
    that never was.

75

We are alive this hour and survive:
     Then, walk with me alone an orchard mile
     Into the twilight end of Conord days,
     Know in my face the acquiescent smile,
     Dissension always deepest in mild gaze
     To look down darkness toward the trembling light—

Prince Arthur
in the Tower:
No more the
eyes of youth.

          Lights out! and the globe broken, and with hot
               irons
          Put out both mine eyes?,
          Still gaze toward music where the light
          Was and the song:
                    Swing chariot philomel in midnight skies!

The last
memory
of Europe.

          Broken, yet not unheard.
                         Say in my heart I am
          That angry ancient legend of a bird
          Who walked alive
                         eating the ashes of his funeral urn,
          Alive to walk until the memory fails
          In clapboard lecture halls.

Phoenix.   O my America,
          And not to speak of you except in praise,
          The midland ocean at my heart,
          Thou art Atlantis risen from the seas,
          Bride of the Indian Summer and the corn,
          The mountain forest, slow, unwinding plain:
          The many footed cities at thy side. . . .

I am thy husband to divorce thee never:
Never-forever is a long, long time
For faith in blindness and the memory gone.

This place an orchard and no roads,
Yet every step I take shall be my own

Till houses fall in houses, cities fall:
Still floats the wedding caul, the oversoul,
My name the hydrographic written on
This stone that crumbles with the garden wall.

　　　Cheerful, the actual smile is permanent,
　　　I turn my head always to face the sun."

Eight

The Meek Shall Disinherit the Earth.

Darkness in rain:
traffic in asphalt mirrors on the Square
gathers before it mounts Fifth Avenue
north through the white-arc'd Victory in stone
toward Five O'clock.
          A voice in air:
"Come talk to me at 61, my attic
an antique stairway-landing in the sky:
'Loaf and invite the soul,' the deer that strays
into our hands, the silver beast
with wary, child-like eyes, yet innocent—
we'll talk until another day's begun."

And through the rain I saw his house loom up,
an old ship harbored into alien time,
dry-docked in broken timber, the bricks fallen,
steel hawsers giving way, the cornice sprung:
and as one stepped inside, one heard the wind.
I saw him leaning from the top-flight floor:
"I have been ill, been poor, yet when night enters
this room that holds the hours I lie awake,
something like youth returns: there is a tumult
of warmth within my veins . . . and then the tide,
music inspired by a golden bird—
that winged bough whose day is always spring
whose fiery chariot is the song unheard
leaping the ashes of Time's Illium
from dark to dark, that lives in fire,
climbs fire that flames upon an iron tree,

takes flight within a dream,
and is the hurricane in deepening calm.

I sometimes feel that I have lived forever in this room:
the rent unpaid, yet I am fed and watered
like a geranium on that window sill—
by landlady, charwoman, or foolish girl
who disappears at noon
leaving her alms behind.
But if I leave the room, wherever I go
I hear a whisper: 'Don't come again;
your face is too well known:
you are Herman Melville of the Customs House,
bright in oblivion and yet unseen.'

In a far reach of the room I sometimes hear
Shakespeare and Dante risen from the shades:
perpetual oak and olive sheltering
the delicate laurel of middle-aged spring,
May in October and an early frost:
the grasses changed to glittering white hair.
No, I'm not bitter: I am always friendly.
I always threaten meekness everywhere,
my face the preternaturally calm
forgiving smile . . .
                Last night I saw a flame
pour out of darkness over eastern heavens:
the earth had perished on the farther shore,
an ocean wilderness on either hand . . .
The sound of that sea shall be my requiem."

Nine

They found him sitting in a chair:
continual and rigid ease
poured downward through his lips and heart,
entered his veins and spread until
paralysis possessed his knees.

The evanescent liquid still
bubbling overflows the glass;
and no one hears the telephone
ringing while friends and strangers pass.

Call taxis, wake the coroner,
police: the young ex-millionaire
is dead.
          Examine unpaid bills—
insurance blanks and cheques unfold
from refuse in a right-hand drawer
to read before the body's cold,
lifelike, resembling what we were:
erect, alert, the sun-tanned head.
Polo or golf this afternoon,
and night, the country club or bar?
"Drink Death to end all poverty:
two millions gone—
                         and stir no more."

Because I know his kind too well
I knew his fears—and the release
of energy that thinned his blood
was no certificate of peace,
but like communiques in war.

The startled Scapegoat sought his way
to safe oblivion that lured him,
made his life intact, immured
his debts and tricked old friends.

I hear his voice: I wake to hear
storm-tilted echoes of his name.
It is his death again: the same
sleek ambulance throbs at his door.

Ten

Yet bring us no more fear:
The empty heart and the closed lung,
The broken song.
                    Perhaps no one will hear
Me when I say, 'It is impossible to die.'
I have seen men starve at street corners in rain
(My face reflected in each eye,
The soul's glass inward down the vertebrae.)

But there are things unsaid that I must find
Written across the bottom of my brain
In night-long memories . . .
                    Praise girls and men
Who shall survive, outface despair
Of the million poor, steel-staved and broken—
Who build new fires at an empty hearth
To burn through darkest hours
Of restless peace and reawakened wars,
To burn away terror and hate,
Old doubts and fears.

Eleven

Under cool skies, Wisconsin's April weather,
Promise of lilac fragrance in the air,
And that vast Lake where memories restore
Westward the wave to India, the passage
Chartered through night
                               and the returning dawn:
Over the mast-head shines the morning star.

Gather, foregather
                          in the pale mist of Juneau's city:
Below it flows the thin Menomenee
Where forests were: clay-banked the silver river,
The trail in memory across the plain.

And from grey roots, the lilac flowering
In tombs that open when remembered spring
Comes home again beneath a tall roof-tree.

And through the night one hears
Disparate voices
Across white beaches, out of shifting waves:
The sound of water leaping in the dark:
The shadowy presence of the inland sea.

Twelve

Among the shades I heard my father's father:
"I am a tall man, handsome for my years:
Astute, four score and ten, my six foot three
Mounting to steer the horses beggars ride,
Ex-Dubliner, astronomer, engineer
From thick green growing turf where I was born
Where blackbird armies wheeled down from the clouds
Breaking the sky through fractured sunlit rain
Until the violet long archaic twilight
Empties its shadows over hill and plain.
I built my bridges to oblivion
Even here across young lakes, across the sea . . .
Get out of my grave: there is nothing here—
Take your hands away—I want none of you: sons,
Grandsons, cousins and fools.
                              Put the spade aside,
No treasures here: the inhabitant's gone,
Nor nakedness, nor sins, nor flesh, nor worms,
Nor rings, nor jewels, nor gold.
The grave has a clever way of keeping secrets,
Everything lost in dust and a few odd bones:
And the last pawn-tickets dust,
And long lost ancestors in deeper dust
Under the green-mossed ruins of family pride.
Be careful with that spade. It is made of iron:
It awakes destruction.
If ever there is another resurrection,
I have the great cold strength to stand alone."

FORTUNE
FOR MIRABEL

(1941)

NANCY HYDE GREGORY

AND

JAMES HENRY GREGORY

Fortune for Mirabel

I

Tell, tell our fortune, Mirabel,
Shuffle the pack and cut
Cards spread face upward on the carpet
Over the faded green sweet and violet pastures:
The hourglass, time, the blonde girl and brunette.
Give us good cards tonight: the faces
Beautiful and new—and love, Mirabel,
The pink heart pierced and the great round yellow sun;
We shall be rich tonight: laurels for fame,
The goldmine falling from your right hand,
And O the lute and ribbons and the harp!

—Not the unopened letter nor the blind eye,
Nor the fire card bright as war flowing through Spain,
Nor the lightning card, troopship in storm,
Nor the quick arrow pointing nowhere to the sky.
Not now tonight and not the spotted devil,
The faithless dancing psychiatric patient,
Who wept, always the lover, not the man,
Sold the pawn ticket—not tonight, Mirabel,
Not the deep cypress vista and the urn,
The kidnaped ten-year-old, the head
In pear tree branches and one delicate frosted hand
On the back stairs.
                    —Nor the green island card that means go home
To the dark house with the gas shut off
Where morning papers drop to the floor,
The milkman passes and the landlord waits—not these tonight.

But the bridal card in white, frail blossoms in yellow air,
New homes unlocked, unwept,

The great good fortune sun card shining down.
Is it love, Mirabel, behind the pearly gates?
This last card? Or the black faceless end
Behind each card, the laurels hidden, the dancer dead,
Tonight over and grey light glancing
On tired, powerless sleeping breasts and arms?
Mirabel: Good morning.

2

It was in sunlit evening, Mirabel,
I saw your face, pale and withdrawn,
The green eyes lighting the deeper, greener shade,
Sparrow and poplar shadow on the lawn,
And grey hair, Mirabel, coifed with black lace
Within a silver veil:
Mint leaf and scent of roses on the air,
And the old promise of the skies beyond the hedge
Of that septennial moon which closes summer.

"Mirabel, Mirabel, tell us our misfortunes," cried the birds.
"We have charmed you into the garden from door and street:
Where are your cards?
                              Nor age nor youth nor pride
Should stop you now; we should hear the worst;
Even the Fates, despoiled by what they know,
Think of themselves as young, as beautiful
As you—artless and shy,
Flushed with their graces in a mirrored room,"
But you had grown sulky and would not speak,
And the reddening light of evening poured at your feet.

And silence came (I believe you turned your head),

I saw a figure stand beneath a tree—
Had he been nailed to bare branches before lightning struck?

"He is not Christ," I said,
"The crown he wears is not a crown of thorns;
It is a wheel such as fools wear on dancing holidays;
Your cards and prophecies
Have waked him from the garden of the dead.
I hear him singing, 'Nothing but love,' still more,
"Grape leaf and hellebore
Grow from the glittering tendrils of his hair."

As the storm's darkness fell,
I heard you whispering your beads,
And I knew before darkness came you were in his arms;
There was a black book in your hand
That had dropped to the ground.
"Tell, tell misfortunes," cried the birds,
"There is more to tell";
And where you had walked, I saw the fiery wheel.

3

Mirabel, the sinful Irish, when they die,
Always return to Eire:
There none is lonely; the cold rain beats
In waves against the soul, and moss-green
Angels in deserted gardens stare through the rain
And slowly lift their wings.
                                    It is where
The sirens, whisky-weeping old women, comb grey hair,
Beg for a penny to curse the world,
To wail, to sing. O it is where
Wandering blue tapers burn through fog
Among frail girls clasping their guilty lovers:
White limbs in the moon's light in an empty house,
Eden's sin in rags by day, and at night
The serpent uncoils his desires.
                                    It is on that dark

Island, Mirabel, where the last wheel turns,
Where cards fly into the wind, good fortune and bad,
Speed into storms that ride behind pale suns.
Mirabel, your eyes are lidless, raise your face:
Look at the birds; the swallows wheel like bats
And have nothing to say
While rooks and ravens circle the cold sky.
Mirabel, the spell is cast, turn where you will,
The purple hills still rise, the blackthorn tree
Tears at your sleeve.
                              This is the place
Where the first sight of heaven is a last look at hell;
Perhaps there is grace before morning, Mirabel.

Two Letters from Europe

1

It was the wishing castle that had deceived us:
day-spring at midnight song through every window,
linnet and sparrow,
and from each sill the ivy-circled dawn
waking each day into a last tomorrow,
piercing bell-towered tapestries and halls,
as if we could delay, if not forever,
the hour that leaves no choice
and is the sacrifice of our own blood
in gardens floating green beside the river
and rose-lipped entrances through summer walls.

There we had walked together,
brother and sister, friends and lovers;
and where we turned (it always seemed
we had been running away and yet stood still)
the castle suddenly opened its wide doors
where every welcome was a face in tears,
the endless deep embrace of Cybele,
and from that cavern we heard the voice
of an agèd man who, rising out of earth,
held in his arms the body of his young daughter:
"O face, dear face,
                         O breast, O golden hair."

2

As flares fell from the sky
                         I saw trees' veins
open their withering branches to entwine

the antique shadow of a white-haired, white-limbed man,
and as it spoke, it seemed a hand had lifted
a golden bowl that held September wine:

"Poetry and truth have been my life,
the difficult searching
among rocks, thorns, and all around me
the deceptively innocent gaze
of Nature from the eyes
of a young girl or from the vault
of heaven or from a white rose
staring among the brambles at my feet.
Only the Greeks saw Nature
through the windows of the mind.

I shall no longer tremble, pale as grass,
before the luminous image of what I was,
the young god in a forest of old cities,
breaking through leaf and flower,
through wall and stone,
calling its love to shelter
under its star-reflected breast and loins,
its will, the earth-will, and its blood the dancers
whose fires are lit beyond a moss-grown stair.
Since I have seen the end of a long day
of peace that was the mirror of old wars,
my voice shall echo from another night
and from its tireless, wheeling stars unfold
light within darkness that replies,
                                        more light,
heard from the lips of a last dim, anonymous face,
the child born crying into a naked world."

The Wakeful Hour

"Pour l'enfant, amoureux de cartes et d'estampes,
L'univers est égal à son vaste appétit.
Ah! que le monde est grand à la clarté des lampes!"
—BAUDELAIRE

I saw the country of the sleepless, glancing eye
Where things resemble life.

Even the distant people
Who walk in thin electric mountaintop blue air
Are lifelike here, and over there
Is a valley where slow sheep gaze
At a man's body fallen in grass, and are things seen
As if for the first time and the last,
And are now, as if forever, bright and clear:

The shining husband, straw flower in his lapel,
Enfolds his love's flat breast and quickening side,
And beyond the suburb, a white casino rises,
Gleams like a wedding cake and disappears,
And through the park at evening faces are
Wheeling behind plate glass in limousines;
It is a vision of life within motion,
Volition within life
That has no beginning and no end
And is always near.

Beneath the floodlit tower clock
A lost child with a sailboat under his arm
Stares at the time. And at his side an old man on a bench
Faces the river where the factories are

Until light fails and a far window opens like a pale wishing star
Blank bedroom walls where two naked lovers quarrel.

In a wakeful hour I almost hear
Noise of lost cattle in a trampled field,
The husband's voice, the laughter of the bride,
Gear-shift of motors through the park,
Boy's cry and factory whistle,
The scream, the thrust of a body against the wall—
And if one saw them as one might see them in a mirror
Move, dissolve in night and reappear,
That would be life itself and always there.
I have heard that the ancients saw them in a circle
From light to darkness, darkness to light again,
Seen through the branches of a golden tree.

They stand between me and the unseeing, unlearned, unknowl-
    edgeable world.
I wear them as a man might wear a shield.

Mutum Est Pictura Poema

"Do not curse me:
                        It was my friend
who framed these sketches
of dying tulips in a glass,
of potted rosetrees, and a street scene
that might be Alexandria or Venice
or New Orleans or perhaps an unfamiliar
noon-struck vision of an overnight hotel
at Niagara Falls.

It was she
who locked my spirit within white,
staring, mausoleum walls.

It was not I
who was unthoughtful or unkind,
but she who sought to justify
love by another name,
to call it art and reverence and fame,
and not that living thing,
voiceless and blind,
that prays for solace in an empty bed.

I had been a good child always, had obeyed
teacher, father, mother;
if she could have taken me from what I was,
and if I could have said,
Open my heart: it is the place where hell is,
you would not be looking at these pastels
nor at that sleeping girl who seems to wear
at her right side a mutilated hand,
nor at these pale and drifting water-lilies."

Look at Me

"ERECTED TO THE MEMORY OF AN AMIABLE CHILD
ST. CLAIRE POLLOCK DIED 15 JULY 1797 IN THE
FIFTH YEAR OF HIS AGE"

—Inscription on a monument at 124th Street and Riverside Drive

Look at me standing fearless in cold and shifting sweet March air:
I am the hope of what I might have been, popular, eager, quick
    and fair;
The truthful son, his wide stare naming birds, trees, flowers; the
    irresistible lover;
The boxer happy, first round won; the careful husband on a Sun-
    day morning; the heroic
Admiral, king, chief, president; the benevolent, sleepless
    millionaire.

I am everything my people wish to be: the perfect child, its
    future still unknown.
See me, cheerful and bright, the eternal, unbroken
Gaze from blue eyes and my head wreathed with wind-flown and
    golden, thin hair,
The invisible light within light,
And the deep smile engraved upon stone.

Four Monologues from
The Passion of M'Phail

I

Do I have to prove I can sell anything?
You can see it in my eyes, the way I brush my hair,
even when I need a drink and can't stop talking.

Do I have to prove it with my two hands and arms,
lifting five hundred pounds above my head,
until the house cheers and something falls,
the platform broken and the lights gone out,
a child calling for its mother down the aisles?

If the park is beautiful and the day is warm,
I can sell the power in my eyes that makes life grow
where not even one blade of grass has grown before,
that is like sunlight breaking through
darkness in a small room,
that shines and pours and flows,
that is here forever when it is here
and is gone forever as sunlight drops to darkness
when it goes.

I could even teach millions how to sell,
how to own a car and pay the rent,
how to live as though you were living in the sky,
your children happy before they get too old.
If you do it right, you can sell anything,
even your voice and what you think you hear,
even your face on billboards ten feet high,
your youth, your age and what you hate and love,
and it gets sold.

If you can wake up in the morning early,
if you can teach yourself to catch the train,
if you can hang out everything for sale,
if you can say, "I am a man,
I can sell asphalt off the street,
I can sell snowbright
dead women gleaming through shop windows,
or diamond horseshoe naked dancing girls,
or eight hours on my feet,
or twenty years of talk in telephones,
or fifty years behind a desk"—
you need not fail.

If you are strong as I am, you can hear
yourself talking to yourself at night
until your hair turns grey:
"I am God's white-haired boy,
I almost love the way I sell
my lips, my blood, my heart: and leave them there,
and no one else can sell such pity and such glory,
such light, such hope
                          even down to the last magnificent,
half-forgotten love affair."
Perhaps only I can do it as it should be done,
selling what remains, yet knowing that a last
day will come and a last half-hour,
or five minutes left impossible to sell,
the last more valuable than all the rest.

2

The lunchroom bus boy who looked like Orson Welles,
Romeo, Brutus, and a man from Mars in his two eyes,
the bellhop who was Joe Louis to the life,
the Greek fruit peddler who in church on Sundays

was a lightning-struck dead image of J. P. Morgan,
the Italian barber who in a mirror was more like
John Barrymore than Barrymore himself,
the Woolworth demonstration cold-cream girl
who was Garbo at a glance, only more real,
the shoe clerk who in midnight rain outside of Lindy's
should have been Clark Gable,
the Second Avenue ex-Baptist minister
who was born to have a face like Cordell Hull's—
why do they look at me like that,
why do they stare,
                              sleepwalking through my dreams?
What was the big mistake?

They looked like power and fame,
like love, like everything you need;
and you would think their looks would put them where
they could dictate a letter or run a bank
or kiss a microphone or float a yacht or sleep in
a genuine imitation Marie Antoinette bed
or get somewhere before they die
instead of dropping into dreams too deep
to tell themselves who, what, or where they are
until a fire turns them out into the street
or a shot is heard and the police are at the door.

3

Sweepstake invisible but real,
somewhere the million dollars
in a vest pocket bank book, dresser drawer,
bills, change: silver and nickel, copper, tin
between your fingers, in your clothes,
on chairs, on tables, rolling on the floor;
somebody's rich tonight.

Somebody's stepping high
foot on the gas, asking for more
what have you got? More anything,
more face, more arms, more hands
big to hold sweepstake honors, the returns
invisible except
here in the paper Blond Baby or The Tuscaloosa Kid
gets the reward,
knowing it doesn't pay to work no more,
until your hands grow cold
and skin turns grey,
body split through and green,
green as a green glass bottle that's thrown away.
Invisible sweepstake, but somewhere on earth real,
the little horse on a white circle trotting
clean limbs to victory
               and spent,
the eyes still bright, insensible, lighting
the darkness of a stall.
Here is no dream, but happiness leans over
like the sight of God
to Broadway Jones or Harlem John
waiting for hope (like love) here for an hour
invisible, then gone.

4

When you are caught breathless in an empty station,
and silence tells you that the train is gone
as though it were something for which
you alone were not prepared,
and yet was here and could not be denied;
when you whisper, "Why was I late, what have I done?"
you know the waiting hour is at your side.

If the time becomes your own, you need not fear it;
if you can tell yourself the hour is not
the thing that takes you when you sit
staring through clinic waiting-room white walls
into the blank blue northern sky
frozen a quarter-mile above the street,
and you are held there by your veins and nerves,
spreading and grasping as a grapevine curves
through the arms and back of
an enameled iron riverside park seat,
you need not think, Why must I wait
until the doctors say:
                          "We have come to lock you up.
It's the psychology of things that has got you down;
if you complain, we shall take care of you
until you know at least you can't escape.
                                          Is your dream

the dream of a child kept after school
made to write a hundred times
what three times seven means,
while in your sleep, before you get the answer,
the blackness fills and swells with pictures
of Technicolor ink-stained butterflies?
                                      Is that ink-blot a tiger

in a bonfire? Are these the spines
of ancient caterpillars?
Is this the shadow of a wild-wood, leaping deer?
Is that what you see, or what you think you see?
Then we can tell you what you are,
what you can do, and what you ought to be,
as though your life were written down in court,
your name the last word on a questionnaire.
There is nothing private that we do not know;
you can't deny these figures on a chart
that follow you no matter where you go.

Each zero is an open, sleepless eye
piercing the hidden chambers of the heart,
and if you fail, or if you kill yourself,
we shall know why."

It is when the waiting forces you to stop
in stillness that you wish would not return
that you say, "I am not the same as other men;
I must live to wake beyond the fears of hope
into an hour that does not quite arrive...."

And in that quiet, lost in space, almost remember
the difficult, new-born creature you once were,
in love with all the wonders of the world,
seeing a girl step, white and glittering as a fountain,
into cool evening air,
knowing you could not touch her,
nor dare to still the floating, flawless motion
of that pale dress above its glancing knees,
brief as the sight of sun on Easter morning
dancing its joy of earth and spring and heaven
over the sleeping bodies of men in cities
and between the branches of the tallest trees.

It is then you tell yourself:
"Everything I live for is not quite lost,"
even if you've waited someplace far too long:
if you can't call it peace, you call it rest;
if you can't call it luck, you call it fate,
you then know that when anything goes wrong,
perhaps it also happened in the past.

You light a cigarette, you carefully
blow out the match.
                    You know again you have to wait.

The Postman's Bell
Is Answered Everywhere

God and the devil in these letters,
stored in tin trunks, tossed in wastebaskets,
or ticketed away in office files:
love, hate and business, mimeographed sheets, circulars,
bills of lading, official communiques,
accounts rendered, even the anonymous letter says,
Do not forget.

And in that long list: Dean Swift to Stella,
Walpole to Hannah More, Carlyle to Jane.
And what were Caesar's Gallic Wars other than letters
of credit for future empire?

                        Do not forget me,
I shall wear laurels to face the world;
you shall remember the head in bronze,
profile on coin.

As the bell rings, here is the morning paper and more letters:
the postmark, 10 P.M. "It is an effort
for me to write; I have grown older.
I have two daughters and a son and business prospers,
but my hair is white. Why can't we meet for lunch?
It has been a long time since we met;
I doubt if you would know me, if you glanced quickly
at my overcoat and hat and saw them vanish
in a crowded street. . . ."
Or at another door," . . . O you must not forget
you held me in your arms, while the small room

trembled in darkness; do you recall the slender, violet
dawn between the trees next morning through the park?
Since I'm a woman, how can I unlearn
the arts of love within a single hour;
how can I close my eyes before a mirror,
believe I am not wanted, that hands, lips, breast
are merely deeper shadows behind the door
where all is dark? . . ."

Or, "Forgive me if I intrude, the dream I had
last night was of your face; it was a child's face,
wreathed with the sun's hair, or pale in moonlight,
more of a child than woman, it followed me
wherever I looked, pierced everything I saw,
proved that you could not leave me, that I am always
at your side. . . ."

Or, "I alone am responsible for my own death" or,
"I am White, Christian, Unmarried, 21," or, "I am happy to accept
your invitation," or, "Remember that evening at the Savoy-Plaza,"
or, "It was I who saw the fall of France."

As letters are put aside, another bell
rings in another day; it is, perhaps, not too late to remember
the words that leave you naked in their sight,
the warning, "You have not forgotten me;
these lines were written by an unseen hand
twelve hours ago, do not reply at this address, these are the last
    words I shall write."

Daemon and Lectern
and a Life-Size Mirror

For God's sake, do not explain that picture
of the bright-haired girl on a diamond black horse,
nor the stilled eyes of imperishable Greek ladies
carefully undressing before a life-size mirror

Let us be glad that we cannot discover
daemon or child who made them, that these realities
of delight and beauty at their imperfect source
are indiscreet, if not indecent, subjects for any lecture.

THE DOOR IN
THE DESERT

(1951)

FOR PATRICK BOLTON GREGORY

A Temptation of Odysseus

I know that island:
It is a garden, and beyond hedge and sea wall—
It is a singing forest of young girls,
Their faces roses, their hands, arms, shoulders
Foam against rocks, white as the throats
Of lilies, girls stepping out of trees,
Walking, as if created out of air,
From willow branches and waterfalls,
From springs and fountains.

There I could whisper,
Look at the languorous one, that creature
Who shakes the sun's hair out of her eyes;
She is the light that moves
Among dark ferns and grasses. She has opened her lips
And is about to sing. I doubt if
What is heard is music—but O that pale
Forehead and lovely shoulder.

And with her is one
Who has midnight in her glances,
Nubian quiet in her eyes where a man enters,
Is drawn, is held as a child is carried,
Sleeping, within four corners of a dream,
The rooms where ash and laurel lift their branches,
And shades of one who killed the Minotaur
Beckon and disappear.

That island is a place
Famous for the noises of its waves,
Bird-calls, cave-echoes, storms of ancient sky

Which are transmuted into the sound
Of girlish voices, a spell that entrances
The lonely man (God help him) lost at sea.
Even learned mariners and snow-bearded captains
Have not been immune—who did not trouble
To hear the meaning of words or score;
They welcomed lightning and reef,
Shipwreck and shallows, the naked beach
Where the tropical island is a threshold
Into dawn.

It was true
I stopped my ears against the singing,
But the secret is: I had closed my eyes
To keep the island out of heart, hope, mind:
If I heard anything it was the shrill
Of peacocks.

It was then I knew
That all my men would leave me; the ship was gone,
They were free to enjoy the quickened dark, the rescue,
The wild embraces, the songs, the shrieks, the laughter.
It was useless to threaten them
With chains and galleys and the loss of home.
They were free of the lot of those who die in irons;
The Fates had given them a sailor's choice
That is reserved for the young, the gay,
The ignorant whose blood is wine,
Whose bones are salt for sirens.

I know that island
As if it were the Zodiac at night
Shining within the palm of my right hand.

Homage to Circe

Lady, the glass you lift has sleep's bright fever in it,
Amber and floating peace within a place
Where he who drinks cannot expect to hear
The throbbing of the skies, the watchful flight
Of wings above his head, nor guide sea-traffic
Through a crowded street.
                              Lion, dog, or swine,
He is a cheerful patient,
Ready to give till he has nothing left to take—
It is the fever that inspires his rosy look.

Lady, you have that rosy look,
Lips shaped as though about to speak, to sing;
Is the fever hot or cold? Do eyelids close forever
In the depths of the fever,
And through the sky-borne arches do sea-bells ring?
Whose are those delicate arms that reach to hold us
Through plate-glass halls where glittering in mid-air
The body rests, and each revolving mirror
Reflects a sleeping mongrel at his ease?
Is this the place of miraculous hotels,
The forest feast embracing us with branches
Where all the rosiest ladies turn to trees?

Lady, your precious glass cannot tell time,
But is of an hour that is forever gone;
Even for your sake its light will not return,
Nor farewells spoken with a gliding smile—
Lady, our journey has outstepped your spell,
We have destinations beyond your kind distractions:
We have passed, are passing

To the sober shores of hell;
It is cold among the waters of the dead,
A less feverish province than the animal kingdom
That is always at your side.
                              We have found no haven,
And our long night has just begun,
Though Hades opens like a winter sky;
In darkness we are closer to the sun."

Haunted Odysseus:
The Last Testament

Do you see them? I mean the Dead:
They have come back again; I feel them walking
About the room, and a face has entered
Through that closed door.

                  I have seen them rising
In fountains out of rocks, the unwept slain,
The green moon-shadow on white breasts and thighs,
And heard their raining voices in the wind;
I saw pale hair
Floating in golden waves against the dark,
I saw hands reaching toward invisible fruit
That once had dropped through summer's heat
Above them.

          This was in their country,
The Palace of the Dead, snow falling as crystals fall
From a dark sky. I heard the sound
Of thick waters moving against rocks, the shore;
Their houses had been burned by fires
Greater than the sun: there were blackened walls,
Each hearth, each portal
Open in ruins to grey sleet.
I saw a ledge, a handrail and no stair,
Only the deeper darkness and the depth
Of another corridor or pit.

                Then from the shadows
I saw a wavering light and heard,
"My dear, my hope, my love," the light

Spoke to me, and I said, "Mother,
What dream, what evil sent you among these ruins,
Lost as a child is lost
In the mischances of love and war?"

          "Death," she replied,
"I am spirit only; all that was flesh
Is fallen into earth or consumed by fire—
The human fate that waits for all of us
Has little patience for those grown delicate and old.
Then my transparent veins released my spirit
To walk among the unwary, the undone.
I am the vision that speaks to you in sleep;
You cannot hold my shade within your arms,
Even my slightest breath has turned to frost;
It dares not touch you—this is my last
Good night."

     Where the light spoke a star
Shone through the portal and was gone.
My brain clouded with tears; I had forgotten
To ask her of the way back to life.
Then I remembered that a shade
Had stepped between us,
The blinded foreigner from Thebes
Who stood as if a tree grew at my side;
I heard the sound of leaves above my head,
And saw a black bough pointed east.

          Perhaps my escape
Was almost fortuitous. And now at winter's midnight
The Dead are here whispering through snow;
They crowd upon me
Between walls of a room or in a quiet street:
"Mea culpa, mea culpa," from earth or ceiling,
"The fault is our fault, mea culpa, we are to blame;
We are wanderers of Hell in every city,

The faithless, the unloved.
The first cause of our fate is in the stars,
We shall wait for you behind an open door
And in your shadow as you walk the stairs."

Venus and the Lute-Player

That young man—
Thin face, dark eyes in shadow, the blue Venetian
Skies and water below the balcony,
Seen where horizon
Falls into distance over his left shoulder—
Makes music with an art that angels sing.
Such songs have power to wake the moon,
Unveil her sleep and draw her from the skies
To walk with him as though she were his bride,
Her light glancing loggia, stairway, stone,
Floating, reflected beneath waters of the canals.

Madrigals,
Songs are flames of Monteverdi
Within the lute, golden in fire as darkness
Turns to day, and rain to fountains
Dancing in the sun.

And one might think
Such vernal arts would capture Venus,
But there is no likeness to his music in her eyes;
She stares and beckons as though her radiance
Alone were summer's noon, as though she said:
"My hairs are golden wires, and what I am
Has been compared to fruits, flowers, vines,
Jewels in the earth,
And the silver motion of the sea—I have no need
Of music nor music's art. I am eternal
Even beyond the sight of artful men.
My presence wakes or sleeps, silent, unsought
Within a darkened room; I need not rise or speak.

I, the world's mistress, remain indifferent
To strings that tremble, to reeds that blow.

                                I am what you seek,
And all you need to know."

Elizabeth at the Piano

It is memory speaking, preternaturally clear,
Awake, remote: the piano playing
Through the dark midwinter afternoon,
The string-filled music at four o'clock,
Chopin, Mozart, Suppé.
                          What I remember
Of that lilac-breathing house
Are flames against dark windows,
And beyond the curtained door
A young girl seated at the square piano.

                    Listen: I hear
The walking metronome: one, two, one, two,
Then the minuet. It is the practice hour,
The pendulum swinging between the walls,
Upstairs and down.
                          There is the smell
Of wet lath, of rain-darkened plaster.

Behind the house the wintry lilac forest,
And behind the coals in the grate
The winter sunset smolders.
                          Is that flame
The sunset breaking through the fire?
One can almost hear the pendulum walk the stairs,
The lonely footfall, then the minuet.

Awake, remote, the house stands in grey-
Clouded brick, leaning through grey midwinter sunset air,
The firelight failing behind the curtained door.
And at the piano in the shadowed room

The dust-filled metronome
Clicks: it is the practice hour.
                              And is that face,
The sunset glancing through darkness
Over white and rose, and caught within
Moonlight of yellow hair, her face?
Is the child there?

Faintly, the minuet—or is that sound a bell
Ringing, unanswered, or someone calling
A child's name down the street?
The house looms, then fades in the wind;
It has begun to snow, the piano is glazed with sleet,
Then frost; it is snowing everywhere.

Statue in the Square

As though I stood at the center of the world,
Grey walls of stone and sky circled the figure
Of bronze-green Dante with its laureled head
Among thorned branches of a winter tree:
"Speak to it," said a voice,
"Speak to that stern, sad, staring face
Which seems to lean out of another time
To this late afternoon, the more than human
Pity and grace as though its light had poured
From sunless skies into this windswept place
Over grey street, park bench and city square."

"Speak to it," said the voice, "even at the hour
When the clock's eye opens upon men at war;
These streets, unlighted windows and black boughs
Are not unfamiliar to its quiet gaze.
Where the ground sighed and spent grasses wept

It has mused upon lost friends and enemies,
It has witnessed and foreseen
Blood on this earth that feeds the roots of trees
And pierced the world into another season
Of day beyond winter, spring, summer, fall
Held in the golden, dream-filled look of a young girl,
Beyond the passion of the grave,
Beyond the last embrace of earth or love."

As I heard the voice, I saw the dark face vanish,
Yet knew its presence in the darker air,
The hand-clasped book, the cloak, the bough, the laurel:
Even though earth fail us and street and city gone,
We shall know that figure and its fiery star
Rising behind the ceaseless sun and moon.

The Alphabet for Joanna

In a child's garden of drawings I came upon a book:
A for the serpent's Apple and wide-winged Albatross;
B was for Bull, Bible and Bell, and "to Be" spoken
In a voice out of a cloud. And there was C, the Cat, coiled in a Chair,
And three-headed Cerberus, the Dog, who stands for D,
Who ate his Dinner in the Dream's shadow
Where water flows behind an unopened Door;
E for the faceless Egg, Easter with dancing suns,
And E for Ermines worn by kings on cards
And guilty, light-haired, pale-eyed player queens.
F for the Fish and Fox, the hooked and trapped,
Floundering and fleet in Flood and over Field,
And G for Grapes and Grass growing beyond a Gate
Where Hills are always H and Heaven and H's are
Horns blowing from Hell's Hearth and fiery Hedges
On Halloweens.

    Then I, thin "I,
Myself walking in mirrors, wide-eyed, and Island
In green glass, speechless and half asleep
Before J, the Judge, in a white collar and a black nightgown
Where Jubal sings beneath a Judas-tree.

      K for King in Kilts,
The gay Kinghorn who sits with a captured princess on his Knee;
L, the caged Lion, from the age of gold
Stares at grey Lazarus risen from the dead
While M, the Man, measures night's Mountains in the Moon,
And N glides near with a great spider's Net
That catches flies where numbed Napoleon stands
In a lead soldier's blackened uniform.

O is the Ocean and Ocarina, the sea and wind,
Orion in the sky and the Oriole's breast;
P is the Pole where weather turns to ice,
And P's are Palaces where Princes stalk at noon
To meet their Queens in Q's that stand in line
To answer Questions: "Is R the Rain?
Or is it Reindeer flying through snow, or Raphael,
Angel who spoke aloud to Adam?"

                    Swifter than S in the Snake,
And brighter than Snake's eyes is Saturn
Burning above the T-crossed earth where T is
The night-wandering Tapir and Targets pierced with darts,
Where Tambourines spin and dance under the bear,
Ursa, and U is Unicorn, the Visitor, V, at night
To lonely Virgins.

                W is the Way, the hidden Walk
Beyond the Wall; X, the unknown, the blue-lighted
X-Ray that shows the skeleton in a darkened glass,
And Y, the Year that runs long June to short December
While Z, the Zodiac, turns its wheel in heaven.

As the book closes, the difficult numerals begin
And multiply in twos and threes and fours,
Yet the alphabet remains where all things live—
The world through open windows and wide doors.

Seascape at Evening: Cape Ann

What is that sound, what is that blue and golden light
Between the rocks, running through grasses,
And at night walking beneath Orion and the moon?
Its colors are in cornflower and honeysuckle,
And wherever one turns, morning or evening,
It is the sea.

        It is the presence
Everywhere: the invisible weeping face
Between the branches of the trees, the ancient
Wild sound between sun and moon, the Doric
Greek return of rock and island:
Voice of the sisters who walk the tide,
Who speak the fortunes of the dead
In salt wind lifting
The pale arms of the sea.

          Even the innocent
Blue flower at our feet stares at us
Through the bright glass of sea and sky,
Speaks to us of the veined rock and the grey forest
Hidden in roots and moss: what does it say
Of lives that have turned to stone?
I hear their voices in the wind, in the waves, in the cries
Of the white-breasted and great-winged
Birds of the sea.

Voices of Heroes

Overheard in a Churchyard Dedicated
to the Memory of 1776

"The cemetery stone New England autumn
Restores health to our voices,
Even our faces
Seem to reappear through gliding mist that gathers
In an unshuttered, moonlit, empty room.
We were the heroes, O wives, mothers, daughters!
Of war that lighted fires
Within these shores.

Open our graves: you will find nothing there
Unlike our common clay
That blows away,
Or mixed with water serves to build a wall;
But you might well imagine
That earth and air
Are relics of the True, Original Cross,
And that the trampled grass
Holds the imprint of Adam's image on this small hill—
Or you might say,
'Because their bones lie here,
The bleak earth glows with sunlight from their eyes;
These are the heroes
And their voices speak among us at their will.'

Yet too much praise leaves much unsaid:
Even in death we were, somehow, more human,
Moving among the shades of things we loved or hated,
Clasping the shadows of pretty girls, or restless women,

Or quarreling with a landlord,
Or gazing with regret at empty bottles,
Or shouldering old rifles,
Or for an hundred years (since we were freed from labor)
Playing at cards with a distrusted neighbor.
It is not true that we were always sad,
Or like evil, unquiet dead misspent our fury
Among cries of death at night in winter storms—
But the earthly spirit that fed our hearts had gone,
Gone with the vanished hope of richer farms,
Or brighter towns, or countless money;
We had learned that there were no stakes to be won,
That the unnamed, vital essence returned to God.

Now that another war flames in the east
(We can see its fires reflected in the sky
And there are more than rumors in the air)
Remember that we died fighting for what you are—
Better to die
Than to sit watching the world die,
Better to sleep and learn at last
That terror and loss
Have not utterly destroyed us,
That even our naked shades
Still looked and talked like men—
That when we wake,
A little courage has earned our right to speak.
Remember that old wars remain unfinished,
As grass grows over earth, our names forgotten,
Or misread, misspelled in ivy-covered stone
With wreaths above our graves in summer's green—
Is that blaze the blaze of lightning from a cloud?
We do not fear them; we know that flesh is mortal
And in a world at war, only the wars live on."

The Blue Waterfall

(Hokusai 1760–1849)

From green heaven to green earth
The blue waterfall: colors
Of spring and summer:
The green-breathing fern and moss
Within pale-lipped rock
And falling water: trees'
Branches golden in light
Against blue water:

              "O river
Of heaven to earth," is a prayer
Said by leaves of the forest,
"Give us your blessing, rain
Into the rivers under
The bridge where the sky
Flows."
        Look, it is there
In the sun; it is the fountain
Wall of blue fires.
            As it is
In heaven, so it is
On earth where the golden goddess
Walks: her face is the sun.

Hokusai, the print-maker,
Stepped out of night
At the fiery center
Of the dragon's eye.
            His eye

Is the eye of the dragon, his hand is
Of sword and sun: it speaks
The will of the goddess: earth, air
And light, her will the blue fountain
Where the woodcutter kneels
To drink of the waters
That are always wine.
                          The green
Earth is awake, the blue waterfall
Is where the goddess
Walks at noon.
                          Hokusai
Is there: his brush made
The fountain, his brush made the prayer
Of the leaves in the forest.
It is always noon.

The Night-Walker

Artemis, Artemis: there is fading
Glory in her net, in the silver
Curtain that falls from sky to street.

Above roof and cornice her face
Returns behind the silver rain;
The ancient huntress walks across night.

Sleepless, she warns and charms,
Sees the new age fallen out of the old,
New ruins where elder cities stood. Indifferent

Is she to these; she has come to warn us
That her pale life, her sterile mountains
Have outlived wars. Her arrows are unspent,

They are still falling in silver light
Above, within the city, their shadows deeper
Than any shelter on the scarred walks of earth.

She is not our being: she is wandering
Artemis who endures beyond life, she is
The light behind a cloud and has deceived
The unwary into an immoderate love of death.

Spyglass

This a spyglass: it
Reads the deepest waters,
Reads the weather, it tells
The time of day, it pierces
Fog and cloud, it searches out
The moon, the sun; it is
A lidless eye, open at morning
And alive at night.

Touch it: even blind senses
Know its ceaseless stare,
How it looks inward to
The dark and how it gazes
Through the outer air

                        It is
The spyglass: it is now
Directed across the plain,
Over a broken bridge, into
The forest, through elm and pine,
Oak leaf and briar, a side of
Rock, a glint of water, the ivy
Vine—careful, the glass is very
Powerful, one can scarcely
Hold it—it has seen
Something that moves, that runs,
Throws itself flat,
Leaps, circles as if shot,
Stands upright, dives, yet cannot
Escape the glass. It is
Running, it has tripped, is

Running, it has grown smaller
Than its shadow, it has lost
Its shadow among the branches,
Among the leaves. The glass
Has caught its face; it is
What we thought it was, not quite
An animal—its pelt is fluttering
In rags—not quite a god;
It is not hard to know what
Its strange features mean;
It falls again; it is
The disappearing man.

In George Sand's Garden

Someone remarked:
"The indecorous lady is no longer there,
Pursued by young and all too faithful lovers;
The print of small feet and the hooves of deer or 'satyrs'
Is not to be discerned among the grasses."
Nor are there signs, among bruised leaves, torn branches,
Of the encounter, almost breathless, and the fall,
As if into earth's center, when the subtle movement
Of the sea is distinctly felt and promises of love
Are overheard among ferns, vines and a sheltering wall
Of roses.

She was neither all heat nor cold:
Her fires were gathered from the autumnal light
Of the moon in her first quarter who seems to walk
Between and above the trees in early evening—
And are as public as the moon,
As quickly turned from cloud-washed gold to silver.
What changeable colors, fragrances, riverlike sounds
And glances entered and vanished
In the illusion of her eyes, of limbs and shoulder,
Of dress and nakedness, and in the green-reflected
Disquiet of her hair.

Even when one saw her
Stride like a man, heard her voice crack,
And knew her veins were filled with a fluid that was not blood,
Was deftly poured, as in a wineglass, for many palates
To taste its salt, to count the beating of her heart
Against the lips, and knew her action
Had less art in it than the command of mind and will—

Even then, among her "rash sorties," the perversions
Of taste, mind, feeling, a less and more
Than human spirit caused a trembling of the leaves,
Sat for the camera, smoking a cigar,
And at the center of a room, draped in soiled linen,
Advised by unpaid physicians and counselors-at-law,
Remained serene.

        Was this, then,
"The Eternal Feminine"? life in short death that "makes us
What we were before"? a metamorphosis
From sex to sex?—so she was read,
Gazed at, applauded, and half, but only half
Forgotten.

        And in her garden, serenity
Is in the summer afternoon, in "nature morte,"
The trimmed lawn, the white and empty marble garden seat,
In skies that open with a blue and vacant stare.
In the sundial, in the distant vista through the trees,
Is the lady there?

The Cage of Voices

Hear them, hear them—all
Of them are back again:
The schoolmaster and the boys
And girls, the white-haired
Middle-aged red face, the faces
Of the young, laughing, laughing,
Laughing behind closed doors,
Or on stairs, or in the hall
Hear them, they know, they tell
All you have done, where
You have been and why;
All are talking, talking
Chattering in the next room.

This is more than a dream:
It is something that is awake
Within a dream; it wakes
And follows you out of bed,
Out of the room, out of the house
And down the street. Hear
Them through an open window,
An open door. Stand in the street
And the shop windows look
At your eyes and hands and what
You wear. They know the secret.

That little girl with the pale
Sharp face and small green eye
Could, if you ask her, tell
Everything: her lips are moving,
She talks in whispers, but an hour

Later, she is a sibyl
Speaking through the walls—
She is merely one of them.
Hear them: they have disguised
Their voices to make you think
They are talking of someone else,
Not you, nor yours, but of
Some other death, some other life;
Yet, if you listen closely,
Closely as when the ear discerns
The stirring of the wind
Within a yellow leaf, or is
Almost certain of a crying
Whisper in the rain—

           You shall hear
Them speak as voices call
In sleep; they have returned
And you must hear.

The Ladder and the Vine

Basalt and coral and gray rock:
This is the portal
Where the dreams walk,
The feathered queen
Who weeps, whose voice is like
The chattering of leaves,
The bird-beaked king
Who glides through dark
Among night-flowering lotus.

> Cypress and olive bloom there,
> Green within green,
> Green within rock and moss
> And the green shadow,
> Quick as a snake
> Behind a child's face
> Smiling in a mirror.
> Look, look into the forest
> Where the sleeper stirs,
> Sighs in the moonless dark
> As the portal closes,
> Green within green, O fastness
> Of the shade and vine.

It is there one feels
The night wind of Avernus,
The darkening silver
Deep-echoing well water
Closing above uplifted hands
And floating hair.
There is no volition

Of hand or shoulder
Within the well,
The faces veiled in green
And shade and vine:
The wheel-eyed Centaur
Embraces sleeping Psyche
Whose lips and folded wings
Breathe within stone.

It is there one hears
The dreams: "We are the voices
Of sleep and shadow
At the shuttered window,
The question heard
At the closed door
Heartbeat and echo
Between trial and answer,
"What is man?" said in the tongue
Of the serpent, 'What is flesh?
What is spirit
That when it leaves the body
Casts no shadow in the sun,
Yet flames in darkness
Of the outer air?' "

"Within the well is our shelter,"
Say the dreams, "all, all
Are sleeping here, body and spirit
Sleeping, and beyond us
Lies the desert where no one comes,
Who dares to enter it?"

And from that waste a voice
Like the voice of Jacob
Cries, "I have seen angels

Rise and fall and call upon me
As though on a ladder
In a pillar of light;
One is wreathed in ashes
From the city of evil,
And the other, fair as the sun,
Stepped from a cloud
As though its will
Were the will of God."

It was in the desert
And from outer darkness
That the third angel came,
Green as the spotted serpent
Clothed in brass.
It was Jacob's spirit
That wrestled self against self
In the eclipse of sun and moon,
That tore and maimed and bled
Till the voice of light was heard
And the desert flowered
And the temple stood.

Basalt and coral and gray rock:
The tongue of the serpent
Is the key
Of both trial and answer.
After the chattering of leaves
Is stilled, heartbeat and echo;
The portal closes and the sleeper wakes,
Turns toward the desert
In the gold eye of heaven.

The Woman Who
Disapproved of Music at the Bar

We heard her speaking of Chinese musicans
And of the house she sold in Westchester;
She said that she could not live there forever
Waiting for things to happen in the mind
Until Martinis entered on a tray,
Or the doorbell rang, or footsteps on the stair
When one was sure the musicians had returned—
Better to live without doctors, lawyers, friends—
And relatives might ask too many questions—
Better to sell everything and move away:
"If I could have said, 'Musicians are gentlemen;
They have asked permission
To rehearse Persephone on the front lawn
Their viols and brasses
Are heard discreetly as the cries, the laughter,
Bird-song and weeping
Of a lonely child who wanders underground,
Her grief, the shadowy spray of maidenhair,
Her joy, the violet in April grasses,'
I could have hired them to play for guests at dinner,
Their music served with sherbets, iced Chianti,
Tinkling behind a plaster cast of Dante,
Echoes, farewells, Stravinsky quieted
Among white roses in a vase,
Glittering between the stems of stained wineglasses.
"It would have been difficult for me to prove
That they were Chinese;
They had come at night, I turned my face away
To the darkness of the wall beside my bed.

I knew that they were there, quite as one knows
That death is in a room, or birth, or love,
Wailing and sighing;
I heard them play
Such music that is heard among the trees,
The sightless music, gong and waterfall,
And I knew that there were faces in the room,
The stone-carved smiling lips and empty eyes
Until I said like someone in a dream,
'I have locked the door: you cannot use my house
As though it were a room in a hotel—
You must let me sleep—
Even if you kill me, the police will come:
There will be blood upon the floor,
A broken chair, torn sheets and footprints in the garden,
And no one shall escape.'

If they had promised
Not to return, I would have stayed,
Have looked each neighbor in the eye and said,
'I have not lied:
There were twenty men among the hollyhocks,
Among sweet peas and oleanders,
And at twelve o'clock they came into my room,
Barefooted, in rags and smelling of the East
As though the earth had opened where they walked.
I was careful not to let them know my name;
I am not responsible for what you may have heard.' "

When the woman left us, one could not have known
That two weeks later
She would actually disappear,
Her phone disconnected, the top-flight suite for rent,
That perhaps the musicians had returned,
Even in the city.
One could not prove that they had followed her.

Police Sergeant Malone
and the Six Dead Drinkers

"My last job was the case of the Six Dead Drinkers:
It has given me dreams and my work is less efficient,
It has shown me the will of death and I am impatient
At the lack of will among those who choose to die,
Even ill-health is a palpable excuse;
I should have dropped the case.

The men were found in a hotel linen closet,
The sixth with a three-inch rope around his neck,
A college student who pretended to be dead,
A fool who whispered
That all youth dies, that he did not wish to live:
All seasons burned for him in hell, he said—
Rimbaud, Rimbaud, Rimbaud!
His breathing corpse was sent to the Polyclinic
Where they brought him to and washed his hands and feet
And offered him the rewards of war and love.

I wrote the first report: it was 'heart-failure,'
Bodies intact and clean, no stains are visible
On wall or floor—
And the victim (if he chooses the occasion)
May wear a judge's gown, or a dinner jacket,
Or the tonneau of a State Department car—
After the police and the mayor are photographed,
Newsmen are always glad to be satisfied.

If the case had been one of gas-house disappearances,
Or a run of phone-booth murders,

Or a Papal Count with an Islip heiress in a lost sedan,
I would have let
The Fairview psychiatrist reclaim the bodies,
For he had said what no one should forget:

                     'These men are not quite gone,
They have merely sunk or drifted past their prime:
Each body is a little overweight,
Regular exercise would have done it no great harm;
There is alcoholic content in its blood,
This one is deaf, the other is half-blind,
Another has a scar on its right side
And still another lacks an index finger,
Which is sad, but each can be beautifully repaired,
Therapy works wonders for such common ills.
They could weave baskets, or model images in clay,
Dye wool, or trace a pattern on a loom,
Or even calcimine the clinic walls—
Each could be salvaged and each could earn
A minimum of fifty cents a day.

But I had my way; I restored them as they were,
Each in the closet as though sitting in a bar,
Friendly, about to speak:
One looked like a schoolteacher with a glass eye,
Another like a teller in a bank,
Another like a sailor, reefed and spent
On an East River barge, one like a millionaire
Who had been reported missing for a week;
And the last with his smile rolled upward to the ceiling
Might have been a correspondent in the First World War.

Like one possessed, I sat down among them to hear them talk,
The door closed quietly and the night was dark:
I felt the cold, stilled air against my face,

I knew the danger, I knew how deeply
Sleep flows among the dead, how straight, how far
The unseen distance falls, my body shaking
And held upon a narrow ledge.

I awoke to throbbing airdromes in the sky,
The nurse above me said:

                    'You must lie quiet,
You have been telling me secrets for days, for hours,
Throat scorched, lips black and your tongue burning;
You have told them all, there is nothing more to say.'

But even as I woke, I could not stop:
There were years more to tell
Of misspent childhoods in the sun at Santa Fe,
Or ten days with a duchess on the Matterhorn,
Or minute views of the Louvre from Eiffel Tower,
Bomb-scares in Jermyn Street, tear-gas in Wilhelmstrasse,
Male sleeping beauty contests at Marseilles—
All, all were there,
Even to the least detail,
Memories of girls with the Indian Ocean in their eyes,
And night-breathing oleander in dark hair,
Words flowing from the lips that could not keep still—
Were there five men in that place, or six, or seven
Whispering my life, or theirs?
I did not know,
I knew only that a phosphorescent, blue-lighted river
Coursed through my veins, that I must talk as if forever
Of everything I had done, or hoped to do.

It was no wonder my recovery was slow,
That I enlisted to begin my life again, to leave the city.
I have heard artillery encourages silence among men—

If they sing, dance, shout or whisper, it does not matter,
The guns speak for them and the sirens blow—
The service leaves no mysteries unsolved;
I have volunteered—
                                    and I am wild to go."

A Foreigner
Comes to Earth on Boston Common

In the shadow of Old South Church the turn of spring is
Slow, melancholy rain from eaves and branches:
There is the smell of clay that once had been
Eyes fearing heaven, hair delicate to touch,
Lips that almost parted to drink, to weep, to smile.

                                        It is reported
One can hear voices running through the grasses,
And at evening whinnying between brick walls.
There, as rain falls, the text is found:
"Vanity," saith the Preacher, "is a rainbow
Glittering against clouds that are filled with tears,
Fold within fold,
Coral in amber, emerald in amethyst,
And is the arc of that crystal ball which is the world."

                                        Sunset discovered
A figure standing between trees and traffic
Unmindful of the dark behind the Common,
Or of approaching night, or of draughts and storms;
He stood as though he felt
The noon of summer in his heart and the sun streaming
Within the veins of his thin arms.

                                        One could almost hear
His fingers call the birds,
Striking and straying, as if they tuned a violin,
Invisible strings of music in the air:
"Sister Water, Brother Fire,

144

Earth and her Seasons whose lips are roses,
Whose breasts are lilies;
Welcome all creatures in flowery dress,
And in thy circle bring pale Bodily Death
Who walks like a woman weeping behind her veils
And gathers the living with her under grass."

Then to him came
A multitude of wrens, the jade-green parakeet,
Wild dove, hawk-sparrow, the flickering
Virginian nightingale, the mothlike Dusty Miller
Flying and fluttering to his knees and shoulders.
When the wings stilled, he began to tell them
Of trees that grew barren at the top,
Of towers that suddenly filled with light, then fell to ashes,
Of the capricious laws of birds and men,
Of the circular blue and golden joys of heaven.

After the birds had flown,
Those who saw him spoke of his archaic head,
Thin nostrils, dark face and transparent body
That rose in air through which night gleamed and stirred.

One had heard him say:
"To see the world without profit or grief
One must lean into it as through an open window;
Waterfalls and rocks abound there,
Flowers and vines, meadows of wheat,
White alps and purple valleys—
After that vision, the grey Serpent who drinks the ocean
And eats the heart and mind
Is nothing but a dream."

It was agreed
That what he saw could not resemble Boston:
He had talked of meeting angels in the street,

Of a flaming bush that could not have grown
In Copley Square. Some said it was fortunate
That he did not return; others that birds have not been known
To sing praises of men. It was clear that no one but a saint
Could speak as he did and not have his eyes
Plucked out by nervous crows.

Opera, Opera!

What work is that?

An Investigator speaks:

"It had been discovered that lenses
Of opera glasses could not be controlled;
They had been cased in mother-of-pearl
And jewelers called them 'a scientific work of art,'
Glittering to look at in the fluorescent glare
Of a salesman's eye, but when one touched them
The hand became unsteady, and the sight
(If one saw anything at all) became
Unnaturally clear.

A box-holder reported
That he saw Valkyrie riding through the lens,
That he could count October falling tears
Of Orpheus raining in a painted forest
Through autumn leaves and papier-mâché towers,
Grey twilight billowing in canvas skies;
He said he could almost hear the chiming choirs
Of angels with tinseled hair and violet wings
Who gazed at heaven with mediterranean eyes,
That when the lens
Pierced the asbestos curtain,
At last he knew that something had gone wrong .

The lens showed Parsifal,
His hairy legs and arms wrapped in a bathrobe:
The box-holder saw the hero stir
Patented headache powders in a cup;
In the Green Room he saw

The woman who was once Eurydice,
Naked as Eve with Adam at her side,
Kiss the reflection of her lips within a mirror.
It was then he noticed that the house was empty,
That the galleries were dark and all the faces gone.
It was as though he had fallen into a cave,
And he felt the invisible shadow of Anubis
Walk through the aisles. He almost wept
And then discovered a nightwatchman
Who unlocked an exit, hailed a cab
And sent him home.

                                    Another victim
Said the lens viewed nothing but history:
Elephants that crossed the Alps in snow,
Winged chandeliers from the Congress of Vienna,
Coiled in smoke, torn volumes
Of civil law and economics,
Rocks among blackened stumps of trees,
Foreshortened deserts and a broken cornice
Where someone carved:
'Voice of the people is the Voice of God—Hail Caesar!'

                                    Another said
That the glasses had been given to a child
Who hoped to see, green as a billiard table
A baseball diamond hidden
In the park, but grew impatient,
Lifted the lens at bedside to the moon
And through a window saw concentric circles
Wheel into a grey sphere with night unrolled behind it;
The boy cried, 'That thing is the face of death,'
The Ram, the Lion, the Archer had disappeared,
Nor could he find his own elusive star.

                              It was decided
That opera glasses betray the universe,
That the view within the lens was both too near, too far:
If the glasses were 'a work of art,'
They should be destroyed, but if 'scientific,'
The valuable lenses could be brought
Almost to perfection, refined, repolished for expert use
Among ourselves, among friends and enemies
In restless peace and all-pervading war."

The Beggar on the Beach

"I have not come here to talk;
I have come to sit; I have been transplanted
From the cornerstone of a First National Bank
On a windy street to root myself
In pebbles, shells, and sand;
It is my shadow and not my arm
That holds out its fingers in an empty glove
Which might so easily be mistaken for a hand.

My silence is
The unheard cries of those who swim
Where no raft follows, where sails, masts, funnels
Disappear up-ocean into a wave that travels
Eastward beyond the thin horizon line;
At my left shoulder there is a cloud
That gathers into a storm
On a beach-crowded Sunday afternoon—
The cloud my shadow's twin in the tide's swell
Which churns gold waters into lead and silver
At its will.

Tell me my riddle:
I am not a mirage, but a being in flesh
Born of a sea that has neither
Waves nor shore, nor moon, nor star:
That was my misfortune. Have you a better
Fortune? are you forever young, handsome, rich
In friends? poor in fear? happy in doubt?
Sad in nothing? hopeful in dark?
Is that what you are? Or do you burn
As my veins burn with ceaseless heat?

150

Whether you answer me or not,
Even at noon, the disguise I wear
Is the body and rags of legless Kronos
Before God walked the sky. Look at me and his shade
Turns boardwalk holidays into a mile
Of broken bottles and twisted iron
Seen through a grey window in the rain.

            Give it your homage,
The shadow is always here. Now you may drop
Your money in my hat."

The Rehearsal

Gentlemen, as we take our seats
In the darkened house, let us rehearse
The properties of the Western Theater;
Attention: this is item one,
Cloth of the Sun and Moon; it is
The Firmament, see how it glitters—
Life beyond life on earth, and
Beautiful. It has been praised,
Many regret to close their eyes
Upon it, the eternal skyscape
Which seems to wake at morning,
To burn at noon and to unveil
A silver mask at night. We do not
Hear it and yet its changes are
The Music of the Spheres—

                            so much for that.
What of the others? plant life,
Animal life, the earthly spirits?
Item: a Lock of Gilded Hair
From the Head of Venus, a Tree
Of Poisoned Apples, a Yellow Snake,
A Hebrew Maiden and a Naked Man—
We need not name them, they
Have walked out of the sight
Of God; they share our dark-
Ness. Here is a White Hot
Caldron for the Jew, a Chain
Of Dragons and Hell's Mouth,
And St. Sebastian with a weeping
Eye—tears? Four Glassy Tears,

Four Kingly Crowns: Russia,
France, Germany, Spain, a Wreath
Of Smoke, all painted on a curtain;
Behind the curtain, the West Wind,
And in the Wind, Three Cries of Beggars,
The Halt, the Maimed, the Blind.

Gentlemen, this is our Gold, our
Inheritance—even the Gibbet,
The Mask of Folly and the Stake,
The Fall from Grace, the Earthly Power—
We cannot sell it, and though
No actors come, we shall wear it
As tapestry is worn.

                      It is our Europe
To warm us in the cave, protect
Us from heat on the rocks, from
Dark, from flood, from moving mountains
Among ice, the fire of lightning,
The drifting wilderness of snow.

The Unwilling Guest: An Urban Dialogue

—How still, how very still the air is
As though it waited, is still waiting
For the clock to strike. Did you see that shadow
Fall behind the clock, behind the white face
Of the dial?

       —No.

—Will you have a drink?

          —No.

—Another cigarette?

       —No.

—If I lift the curtain I can see
Three Spaniards, a Welsh Albino and a Levantine Greek
Drinking their hearts away. One wears
A newly rented evening gown. I can almost
Hear them singing. Did you say something?

             —No.

—That's half the charm of living
In the city. Do you expect to stay here long?

             —No.

—You must remember it is a holiday: the
Coronation of another half-century,

154

And nearly midnight. The snow is falling lightly,
Carefully drifting, yet the room is very warm:
"You could fancy we were lying
On the beach." Do you want to sing?

                  —No.

—Do you find the room unnaturally quiet?

                       —No. It
Is probably trying to think. If anything waits
For something it cannot think.

—You mean it falls apart? But the room is still
Here. You can sit on the table or pace the floor
Or talk.

        —That is what I meant.

              —Listen,
Is that a starling behind the chimney-piece? Or water flowing?
I forgot to water the statues in the hall,
The three girls picking flowers, the little ones
Called Morning, Noon and Night. And the large ones,
Father and Mother, who sometimes talk,
Should be fed at once, then covered with a cloth
And put to sleep. One becomes extremely
Domestic if one lives alone.

             —That fluttering
Of wings behind the walls could be echoes
Of a blind man playing a violin,
Or is everyone in the city blessed with eyes?
You needn't answer.

155

       —There is a half-domed
Casement pouring light above us; it is not,
But looks like a three-quarter moon.
Would you like to see it?

    —No.

        —If I open the shades
You will see layers and layers of freshly cut
Plate glass, light splintering
The streets from a million windows.
And O the people! Everyone talking, laughing, dining out,
But you cannot hear them. Here is one window
Filled with dancing couples, and in another
Four children are playing cards, and in that window
I think I see a party at a concert:
The usual pearls and gloves, white shirt fronts,
Naked shoulders—and minutely printed on a folded playbill
Held in a woman's hand, Roméo et Juliette.

        And in the windows
Everything to sell: the latest inventions
In copper wire, spun brass, guncotton, steel,
Even uranium, each almost perfect of its kind,
Sharp, clean, reflecting light—O a million lights,
Floodlights out of the dark,
Cross-beamed, white, yellow, red against the sky.
Shall I open our window?

    —No.

       —Everything looks
As it has seemed for almost fifty years,
A trifle overbright, but ingenuous, cheerful,
Mindful of holidays: the Alexandrian city.
Do you remember Alexandria?

156

                            —No.

—Pharos?

            —No.

                —If I draw the shades
It is as peaceful as Pharos before the tower fell.
But we, of course, are on a different island,
Hearing other rumors, if we choose to hear them,
In the African silence of this room.
Shall I unroll a map? There are rumors
That all cities are fires dropped from the sky
In a curious geography of wars:
This shaded portion of the map was Pharos:
The gods no longer walk there.

                        And across the water
The grape withers and runs over
A mound of thistled grass, and look, the Pyramid
Of Cestius is a pillar of smoke.

                        There is nothing here
That the wind cannot blow away, except the harbors,
Except in the deeper forests perhaps
A cave. If you look too closely, the map is
Like a lecture at a museum
That no one cares to hear. Is that shadow still
Wandering behind the clock? Even as you leave the room,
It is still a temporal hour:
It is excellent weather for a holiday.

The Door in the Desert

Red rocks and sand: it was the Haunted Desert,
cliffs, mountains, caves and long-abandoned valleys;
where fires once roared, there was an empty crater;
terror had passed this way; no one returned.

Then came the long plateau into the west;
the grey sky opened like a winding sheet,
half-luminous, half-dark with ancient blood,
and where we looked a voice fell out of air:

"We have gone too far: no more hysteria here!
Eat, kiss, make love, drink cold tea for clear heads,
smile without laughter, bury the dead in trenches
without passion, beg, buy, offer and accept
tomorrow and the next, nothing so cheap
as death, so rare as living . . ."

As we drove farther through that wilderness,
I saw the standing lintel of a house—
all that was left of it, a groundglass door,
and etched in glass a woman feeding swans:

behind her a black-pitted silver mine
under the clouded sky where floorless, broken
a clapboard church leaned slowly through the rain.

The door locked out the furious winds behind it
while the naked, calm Greek woman stared at her swans.

MEDUSA IN

GRAMERCY PARK

(1961)

FOR

MARION MOREHOUSE

AND

EDWARD ESTLIN CUMMINGS

DRAMATIC EPISODES & LYRICS

Boris MacCrearey's Abyss

A Monologue with Two Characters

The characters and the situations are imaginary; they refer to no persons, living or dead.

The scene is a penthouse on Manhattan's East River. The time, fifteen minutes to midnight. The speaker, MacCrearey, clad in dressing gown and slippers, is a bald-headed man approaching seventy. He has a courtroom lawyer's resonant voice; he pleads well, and is obviously used to having his commands obeyed. He does not listen to others, and resting on his ears in the form of greatly enlarged horn-rimmed spectacles is an aid-to-hearing device. The audience faces the three walls he describes in his monologue; as he describes his abyss, he faces the audience, for it is in the region beyond the foolights and where the audience is seated that he feels his abyss exists.

After the first four words of his speech the curtain rises. MacCrearey is seated with his back to the audience, quarter-facing a door (rear right) through which X glides, a young man who might well be a teller in a bank where MacCrearey has his account. He has a teller's nearly speechless poise, broken only by occasional opening and shutting of his mouth as though his lips were forming words. Because MacCrearey would not hear him anyway, he remains soundless throughout, and as the monologue nears its end, slips out of the room as noiselessly as he entered. There is a noise of heavy winds off stage that punctuates the passages of MacCrearey's monologue.

Come in, come *in!*

                 The night above has wings
Strong, black enough to sweep the soul away.
I feel a cyclone lifting iron arbours,
Uprooting bricks and stones.

                     Look out. Your head!
That was a cornice falling through wind gone wild.
Is the door closed?

                Good, the bolt is automatic,
Everything double-locked and sealed, and no bones broken?
I knew you'd come and hoped that you were brave:
The worst is riding up these fifty floors
Through swaying walls and the dark noise of rain
As in a lighted coffin to the landing
To answer my phone call, to rescue me,
Not quite a friend, but someone almost friendly.
No, I'm not ill: perhaps you thought I was:
That was because my voice went shrill and cracked.
My doctor says I must have visitors,—
Even my wife left me and three sons
While I made every effort to be kind:
I always share my wealth with everybody,
Serve drinks to keep them happy, give them presents.
They go away.

                What's that? You say it's late?
When you pace the floor, white nights grow dangerous?
Not yet. This room is safe: the walls insured:
It could be moved into a mountain vault
Where we would sit with office files or jewels,
Secretaries typing notes and food brought in,
Clothes cleaned and pressed and everything in order
As it is here.

             The rent? A trifle more:
The vault a real protection from the weather.

Of course the storm is bad. It always is:
Rain, sleet, snow, ice, and wind that flays the earth:
Each time it's worse than ordinary storms
That came last month, last week, or yesterday.
Storms fifty years ago were mild as brandy,
Scarcely remembered for being storms at all—
Though people lie about them, telling how
Their storms went wild—which is untrue, unproved;
If so, we wouldn't be alive to talk.
Hear that great wind! It makes you feel the rain.
You need a room like this: a welcome home.

Come, here's an introduction to three walls:
One has a sunrise spray of cherry blossoms,
Very expensive with inlays of pearl,
And on its shelf a Chambered Nautilus
To give me hope, but I've forgotten why;
The other has a tropical relief,
An oleander from the South Atlantic
Set back among the maiden ferns at evening
Which after midnight cools the atmosphere;
The next has parakeets who chime the hour,
Useful, yet casual for the parting guest.

But here's the view, the view that's not a wall
That walks for miles. It always moves with me;
There's nothing better than a sheer abyss,
Going down and down and down, close, intimate,
The edge as narrow as my thin left hand,
Yet just beyond hand's reach.
                                        Careful, don't slip!
Of course I wouldn't push you, or myself:
That would be foolish, or unreasonable:
No, not tonight. You're here for safety's sake.
I'm careful as a cat, perhaps too gentle,

Too generous, too sweet, as people say.
My view is welcome wide to visitors,
A park that seems to hold hell's heat in winter.
Deep frost in summer, bottomless, yet here.

There, at our left, a fall of rocks and rivers,
And at our right, great oaks and cypresses
As old as earth that used to climb toward heaven
In mountain-tops and firs to meet the gods.
The farthest vista is a sight of ocean
Rising in ceaselesss waves against the sky—
Which may be Europe, or a glimpse of Asia
At dawn or evening, very far and rare.
If I had binoculars!
                              Yet such machines are useless,
Too astronomical for sights like these.
It's best to take the vista as it is,
Ancient and blurred, but truthful to the eye
Which adds a fourth dimension to the room,
The city washed away like time beneath us,
And nothing there except the perfect view.
Did you say it makes you sick?
                              The air is thin:
It's space we need, and there the prospect flowers
In unclocked time that wakes in sleep that's timeless,
Green mysteries that change our hands to leaves,
Or restless hair to snakes, or tears to amber
Within the green abyss that covers all.
I warn you that you shouldn't lean too far:
Watch me, and look at faces over there
That seem to look at us with lidless eyes.
Before one sees them, one must learn to look
At things that are becoming what they are,
Ex-relatives, perhaps, ex-hopes, ex-childhoods
That walk the green baize lawns of an abyss

164

Down, down that winding path behind the willows,
A place for an accouchement or a murder,
And the grass scarcely stained. It grows again.
That's Nature for you!
                              And because the light is
A clear north light that penetrates the scene,
I've made this spot a weekend studio
Where one may sit for years: to feel, to think.

On summer Sunday evenings when the dark
Floats up in windless air above the city
I see my head rise on a silver screen
The face is Buddha and the smile is Greek
Above the view; its eyes read all the papers:
News of the World in forty languages,
Wars, treaties, fifteen minutes for a drink
To sign the peace before the next war starts.
Do you find the head obsessive? I think it is.
Don't speak now, tell me later.
                              Now, the view:
Directors of museums say they like it,
Like the idea, but not the execution;
They say the brush-work's wrong, a bit naïve,
Last year I had collectors bidding for it,
Three Texas millionaires who wanted culture,
Got tired of breeding cattle for a hobby,
And wished for something big to save the world,
Bigger than churches and something for the future
That might bring profit to their children's children
To make them greater than their ancestors.
Yet it can't be bought.
                              One day I bought a ranch
That looked like it, deep in a canyon, perfect,
Snakes, rabbits lived there like twin brothers, roses
As big as peonies swayed from its walls,

And Mexicans to keep the place in order.
It was ideal. I gave the ranch away
To house a little colony of artists
To make them happy. Then I left them there;
The gates were locked and nothing could disturb them:
They drank, they took in women, killed each other.
Only a few escaped.
                    But have you left the room?
The night is getting earlier than ever:
If you would walk in any house you know,
Outwit the host, and open a closed door,
There's his abyss that drops below a window.
Where are you going? You have gone too soon.
I heard a closing door—or did you fall?
I've shut off power from the elevators;
The stairs are sleek with ice; all lights are out,
And if you leap, there's the abyss or nothing.
O God! that storm!
                    It will be worse tomorrow!

Medusa in Gramercy Park

If you would save me—
                    save these lines, these letters,
Postcards, glazed views of Naples, Nice and Rome.
They are my life, hopes for a further journey,
Souvenirs of action, words dropped from the sky,
Postmarked all hours of night into swift mornings,
Coffee untouched: the time is time to go.

One day: the Rhine below my ivied window,
The glint of water through a green-winged valley:
And there's Cologne! clock turned at half-past noon,
Forests behind me and my watch reset,
Gare Montparnasse with tickets for the Opera,
Time for a short walk as the twilight flickers
Between the White Queens of the Luxembourg.
And in late August—there is Giotto's Tower
Next day: luggage made safe, and the siesta
Banished at three o'clock
                    Did you hear rumours?
Perhaps blackmail?
                    Do not believe that porter:
I tipped the boy five times what he deserved—
Then walked for hours.
                    There I saw the Arno's
Delicate, pale, glass-green arm slipping past
Il Vecchio into dark-ringed southern evenings.
Tired, I sat to rest in bright cafés.
I did not speak to anyone at all,
Nor made appointments for a later meeting:
That's not my way: I act at once—
                    or never,
Never and silence, looking toward the door.

It's true I missed the concert at the Pitti,
Usually bad, and tuned for German tourists,
Bald shopkeepers with whores, hausfraus with students
Pawing each other, half-naked in rear aisles:
Protest, consent within the public darkness.

Then I flew north in rain, the changing season,
Equinox flashing through clouds, and the forced landing
In mile-deep mud, breakfast at airport dawn,
My hotel booked by phone, a wind-slashed taxi,
A cigarette through sleeping Kensington,

Did you hear I'd taken rooms in Bloomsbury?
That news is false, no less preposterous
Than if I'd rented Tudor flats in Rye.

The days had shifted into late September,
Clouds, clouds, then silver sunset through Green Park:
I paid the taxi, walked to find my bearings:
One hundred thousand times I circled past
The splay-winged Eros spawned at Piccadilly,
Impatient at his aim, spent arrows lost
Among the sightless crowd that winds toward home,
None following me, nor sailors, nor kept boys,
Nor blowzy women.
                              Up Regent Street again
To pace shop-windows, and in one doorway
A black East Indian feeding a sick parrot:
'No greater love . . .' I thought, and had to spit,
Then wheeled away.
                              Eros again in twilight,
And crowds dispersed in swifter melting traffic.

—My life, like the life of the wind that turns street corners!
Passion that rises as the wind through empty girders,

Scaffold and spires, then briskly skirts the park,
Rattling the door-pull, thrusting up the knocker,
Pressing the button that wakes electric bells,
And is the vanished hand that slips a letter—
Block-print, misspelled—beneath a door that closes.

Perhaps the lies about me started later:
One's never sure of where a lie's conceived,
In bush, in cellar, or under the back-stairs—
The half-truth's a blind whisper in the bedroom.

Like east Atlantic wind I reached New York
In bright October suns: the flares of autumn
Striding among the trees up Riverside:
Old friends at lunch to meet, forget, renew—
Letters to write.
                    Then I felt gossip sliding
Just out of reach, smiling through cocktail glasses,
Folded in waiters' napkins serving wine,
Or clothed in green plush of the club-room sofa,
Rumours impatient as myself, yet out of hearing.
I felt I needed someone to explain them,
Refute them, or deny.
                        I'd met that woman
Five years ago, the tall, consoling female
Who took one's hand in white companionship,
Held malice in the corner of one eye.
We smiled. I felt we knew the world together:
She, her three husbands happily divorced,
And I, my friends. She would ask nothing of me—
Except odd ends of gossip: the fools we knew,
A brace of theatre tickets, the Ritz Bar—
Myself less intimate.
                        The day was bright—
That was the day I saw her before rumours

Waked up to follow me, the kind of day
One sits with empty forehead to the fire,
Or at a sun-lit window, counts the grains
Of dust that falls in golden multitudes—
Mindless split seconds before time advances—
Again the time to go, and the phone ringing
Anonymous voices through the morning air.

What you have heard is a shrill parody
Of what I might have done, and each detail
Invented by hysterics in a woman
Screaming of rape (or murder) down the stairs.
The truth is difficult enough: it runs away.

It was a Sunday noon. I had walked all morning
And came into a square like squares in London:
An iron-gated park grew at its center,
The staight four sides were partly Regency
Red brick, white columns—partly latter-day
Elegant, though faked, diminished Florentine.
There, over all, a round-faced clock shone down:
It watched me as I moved. I felt its heart-beat
From its grey monolith behind the square.
It might have been a vision, but was not.
It hung like a stilled mirage in the sky—
And I to leave New York within a week.

Suddenly I saw her address on a door:
I rang the bell, leaped up three flights of stairs—
Red runners on the stairs; this I remember—
I forced the door, strode in, the catch undone;
I heard it clatter to the floor behind me.
I saw her in a stream of sunlight standing,
Hair fallen loose, her nightdress in disorder:

One breast uncovered: 'To nurse a child,' I thought.
I was not childish. She was like Medusa
Before the curse fell on her brilliant, white,
Heavy-limbed and still; clear-eyed, she seemed to wait.
The room stood still. Across its mantelpiece
Ceramic apes, dressed in small-clothes, white wigs,
Played bass-viols, fiddles in a *sinfonietta*—
And yet no sound.
                I overturned a table,
Split into rags a chair-hung evening dress,
And tossed shoes, slippers through an open window.
Yet staring, she stood there: her dress had slipped,
And, like a veil, it floated to her feet.
I had not said a word, nor did she speak:
She was too frightened (so I heard) to phone police.
I never touched her; she was free to act—
My actions were the tokens of our friendship,
Of lies, half-truths, bad dreams, humiliations—
I left, silent as ever, my work done.

Caught in a rain of tears, she phoned her friends—
That's what I heard—the rest was pure hysterics.
I'm not romantic enough to say, 'She's evil,'
But rather that she could say anything,
Even deny my visit, say someone else
Had walked into her room, found her defenseless.

I walked the square, impatient at the loss
Of my desire, the wish to see her staring
Blank blue eyes at me, and my eyes the mirror
Of diamond-like reflections of gold hair.
I thought: 'She's old enough to be my mother,'
And by that time, I'd reached Park Avenue,
Bright in the sun, but cold as frosted glass.

It was then I booked my flight to leave New York:
The time to go runs south.
                              I avoid the camera:
Read this and see behind me island tropics,
My shoulders straight and made for epaulettes,
Myself clean-shaved, dressed in duck-whites—all heat—
Lips chaste, eyes firm beneath a broad-brimmed hat.

Effron Siminsky's Afterdinner Speech

The straight, the narrow city, careless goddess,
More boy than woman poised against the night,
And blue-flamed stars reflected through her hair.
The still cold falling from November skies.
Yes, I live here: I'm stranger here myself,
Past master of the second violin,
No one like me: they called me 'Silver Echo'
Because my hair is white—my art a music
Stranger than Prague, or cupids from Vienna,
And you're a stranger?
                          Right! We all live here
On bromal, cigarettes, aspirin, coffee, tea,
Strychnine at dinner—and we call it 'life.'

I have seen the world break open at my feet,
The creatures in it blind, unwary tigers,
Leopards with glass-green eyes, bald-headed peacocks,
Parrots who shout 'Hello' all afternoon,
Grey-haired baboons who try to shake the hands
Of everyone they meet—who weep real tears—

These are the common foreigners, the strangers,
The civilized barbarians of the street,
All colors here: basalt and gold, pink, ochre,
Seals blowing trumpets in an orchestra—
O I have heard a Rocky Mountain bear
Perform *Le Sacre du Printemps* upon a harp.

Wonderful! Then see the creatures glitter,
Stray beggars dressed in rams' wool, ermine, mink,
Attend museums, admire Braque, Kandinsky,

Turn stares at Miro and make eyes at Pollock—
Who wear carnations from a subway platform—
And beg ten dollars for a taxi-fare.

I might say, 'You're a snake; you're skin and dust,
Wear diamonds in bed and pearls at breakfast—
You crawl in dust to beg—' yet I say nothing;
I am polite; I walk the floor; I bow;
I tip the furs a dollar: they stroll away.

And you and I? Strangers, of course, but better,
Better tonight than other strangers are.
How many bromines make the hours of night?
Or two, or four? My wife sleeps five or six—
My sun-tanned bronco wife—built like a boy,
Swears like a boy—'God-damn!' she says,
And grins cats' teeth behind a glass of gin.
Oil—that's her money—half of Oklahoma
In fathers, uncles and an aunt who died:
Her grandfather collected dogs and art,
And she collected me like something ancient,
Something that could be bought, yet not for sale,
Refined, artistic, always European
That takes a whip.
                    Blonde—and a fire in wheels
That burns in ice is what she is—all ice,
Flames in a crystal that cannot break nor melt:
Swift in a Jaguar she goes out camping—
And I, her dog, her art.
                    Now, do you wonder,
I do not play my violin?
                    She saved me
From Widow-in-Black-Landlady on the stair,
Tall as a mountain, holding out her hand,
Waiting for rent in Paris or Mexico.

It is not money, but power that lives in money
That heats the blood and turns the soul to ashes,
Freezes the heart, and changes life to clay,
Invisible spirit against the human spirit:
It's the same power that holds me to this city
Where power flows to steel behind glass doors,
Opens a suite of rooms above the night,
Prisms and chandeliers and silver carpets,
Wax roses and camellias blossoming
In music—no, not music, but great windows
Streaked bright with rain and shining in midair—
A frozen palace where the body sways
Helpless to sleep, to bed.

                It's the same force
That winds midnight to dawn, small hours flying
In chambers of the brain to layers of dust,
The same turn of a sleepless, unseen hand,
The whispering watch in echoes at my wrist.
Do you hear it? I can count them in my veins.
It's earth that's turning.

                Now. You almost hear it.
Don't laugh. I sometimes make myself sound queer—
'Damn queer' my wife said, then she smiled and left me;
She phoned a lawyer, snatched her bag and keys—
A noble woman who makes up her mind,
And nothing changes it—except the wind:
She booked a plane to Europe or Japan.
I wear a fur coat, too—that's alimony
She'll leave me in her will.

                Have you a cheque?
A hundred or five hundred till next week?
Aspirin! Life! No? You're not generous,
Not to musicians? Then, you don't believe me;
You do not see me as I am tonight,

A creature of the sea beyond the harbor,
Past Great South Bay, and off for Labrador—
No shore in sight and all land lights are gone,
New York behind me, and the earth in pawn.

Sisters at the Well

Deborah to Miranda

The curtain rises on a one-room apartment in the upper West Seventies of New York City. The room is cluttered with overweighted 'brown decade' furnishings which include a 'day-bed,' a sofa, glass-faced bookcases, a writing table at which Deborah is seated writing a letter with pen and ink. Behind her is a huge green Chinese screen which has a gold dragon scrawled across it. A green parlor lamp is at Deborah's right side. Deborah, a middle-aged woman with grey hair, completes her letter, sinks back in her chair and closes her eyes. She then switches off the lamp, throwing the stage in darkness, reciting the first seven lines of her letter. With the eighth line, she turns on the light and reads her letter aloud.

Green within green, fastness of shade and vine,
I felt the waters of the well, Miranda,
Rising around me as I put out the light:
The dark room was home again as though time were
Forty-five years ago in new moon's shade,
Clock beating its heart in the cold house,
Gable-cornice-roof-shadow fallen across the lawn—

Across the well, Miranda, where you had gone,
Where you had slipped away to count the stars,
And there saw branches of the house reflected,
The white eaves tremble as attic windows opened
Floating and flowering as a roof-tree flowers
In well-deep midnight circling down
Where silver-tinted fruit falls through Orion,
Tree spreading veins through bright or stormy seasons,

Your body poised between two hemispheres—
O see how closely branches resemble roots
In that round mirror tilted to the sky!

Was it not true the well's eye was God's eye,
The presence that saw Joseph in a pit,
Naked and torn? that looked on water gushing from a rock,
Pouring and coursing in a blessed stream?
That saw—all grace—the King of Egypt's daughter
Bend to the source of waters under earth
As though her eyes had opened on a dream?

So you had run to the well, saw through stilled air
The image of a young girl leaning there,
Flush-tinted breasts, her dark eyes fixed in darkness,
The white limbs quickened with a golden heat,
And bright hair streaming
As though she held a lover in her arms,
Admiring herself in the round mirror
That was the well. She thought herself alone,
But I stood over her, my face as bright, as pale
As the ringed moon on summer Sunday evenings.

From top-flight windows that was what I saw;
I thought, 'Miranda, stolen waters are sweet;
Bread eaten in secret is the soul's delight.'
I knew you would bring a husband to your side,
That the well was the world's well rippling at my feet—
Though it engulf me, I could not enter it;
My blood had turned to ice with prophecy.

Then from an empty steeple I heard a bell
Speak scores and years and days and hours:
'I must step aside,' I thought, 'and my young sister
Must not know what my eyes know, my ears have heard.

Let her take the house, let her drink of the well;
I am she who may betray as she foretells;
My knowledge of that night may work us ill.'

That was why I have not been home for many years,
Took the least inheritance and grew alone.
Miranda, you were a fool, lived naked with a fool,
Got children that were chickens, cats, dogs, mice—
Was one a parakeet? I half forget.
I have outlived my prophecies and tears.
I have lost pity, even for myself;
I shall not harm you; we might live together;
After long years I have nothing to foretell—
When we meet I shall probably speak my songs of praise:
Hope, grief have emptied their waters into the well.

Concerto in Tuscany

For Three Voices: *Announcer, Basso; Baritone; Soprano*

Scene: A clear summer evening in the Piazza of a baroque palace. Carytids support the cornices of three walls right, left and facing the audience. All three voices are in evening clothes. Basso is white-haired, wears white tie and tails. Baritone wears a white raincoat draped across the shoulders of a dinner jacket, black tie; his black suede slippers are dusty. Soprano is in an extremely low-cut evening gown; she is bare-legged and wears high-heeled dusty gilt sandals, which she kicks off as she begins her first speech and remains barefooted until the curtain. Basso, standing in the center of the stage facing audience, speaks with authority throughout the performance.

Basso

Of course the evening waited for a concert:
Cats mewed, dogs barked, and swallows whirled
Over tiles, through rafters; wild clapping
Of wings in air—then antique silence where
Caverns opened to receive the sun. A match
Takes fire from the wind.
                         Through terraced
Corridors I hear stilled voices; in crowds

(He inclines his head in the direction of Baritone and Soprano.)

I see new foreign faces.

180

Baritone

                    Where is the concert?
Where are drums, brasses, piano, flute,
And the first violin? We have come to hear it—
With tickets in our hands.
                    We saw crowds
Gather and we followed them.

Basso

                    From the blue arras
Rose leaves and pollen drift to the floor;
Beyond the garden, clatter of knives, of forks,
Of breaking glass. The feast has passed.
Were *you* invited to it?

Soprano

            I *knew* it!

(*She turns to Baritone.*)

We are too late again—God damn!
                    It is because
We are neither guests nor friends.
                    Where are
The crowds? chairs, love-seats, sofas, tables
Set in aisles across the hall?
                    We have been
Promised music.
            We carry photographs of what
We are—authentic!

(*From her evening gown she extracts a photograph and waves
it in Basso's face. He steps back.*)

            I have a face that *smiles!*

Basso

You must wait!
                    Listen to sounds of evening
Climb the walls, enter a room through closing
Doors—before you hear distinctly what they mean—
You may sit or stand or go away.

Baritone

                    We traveled
Half the world to hear the music. We come—
From homes worn down with boredom, lust, grief,
Divorce, pity for the way we live—tickets
In hand waiting for new music—
                                            music
That tells us what to feel, how to know
What we should know—music to give us
New hope that's not old hope, but waking on
An island, far into night.
                    We have paid for
Arias, duets, concertos, symphonies,
Entire operas, music flowing upward
From wells beneath a house, beneath the floors.
We have bought them. The best seats are ours.

Soprano

Music is love. There is nothing I love so much
As real musicians. I may be foolish, but love,
Even in bed is personal—with me, at least,
Not big and vague and no one—and it
Should be musicians. It must be someone playing
As if the strings would break.
                                    I cannot see
Musicians anywhere.

Baritone

You talk too much.
Keep quiet. They may refuse to give us music.

Basso

There is silence overhead among the clouds:
A city rises from the last rays of the sun,
An Etruscan city of purple hills and vineyards,
Buttresses, watchtowers, the wall surrounded
By fiery lakes, waters of air, of blood-red aether,
Above them earth-colored warriors and gods.

Soprano

We are not welcome here: the other people
Have walked in and taken every seat.
I hope they have not come here to fall asleep—
Such a waste of time!

Basso

                    And from distant hills
There is the sound of rain. Few hear it.

(Backstage a dazzling prism-colored floodlight is switched on.)

Baritone

Someone has lit a curtain behind the palace:
It is a picture trembling in the wind—
It's wonderful to see what culture is—
A dance of centaurs in a painted forest,
And with them girls in obvious distress
Who are drunk, cheering, or in tears.
I never knew that centaurs were like that;
I thought them teachers bearded with great knowledge,

Friends of the young men following Achilles—
I wish I knew the title of that picture.

Basso

It is not 'The Murder of the Innocents,'
But is of deeper, difficult antiquity:
The young women, both willing and distraught,
Are of an earlier fall—and after it,
Laughter in caves, cries among reeds and grasses,
And spent souls walking the grey wilderness.

Soprano

He must be speaking of a bacchanal:
A stupid party where everyone stamps in,
All horses in corral—the strangest people
One wouldn't talk to in the street, women
In big hats: shoulders like football captains'
And feet like horses' feet shaking the floor,
Amazons and centaurs—they all look alike—
Plunging, shouting, upsetting chairs and tables,
Old girls left over from the First World War,
Nasty and loud because they're older, bitter—

Basso

That is not what I said.

(The floodlight backstage dims.)

Baritone

Look at the curtain:
It is beginning to fade.

(Aside in low tones to Soprano.)

184

If you stop talking,
Perhaps they'll give us music. Other people
Are very quiet.

Soprano

Musicians are getting drunk.
Music is love, not drinking.

(Giggling.)

I smell their breath;
They're nasty and I'm thirsty—
Where's a Martini?

Basso

Another scene shows windows to the west:
Tall Venus, the first star: the dark-winged
Cypress leans against the moon . . .
Beneath her path, down shaded hill and valley,
Olive tree and vine asleep in silver mist.

Baritone

I think I hear hoofbeats and sighs, the sounds
Of weeping in the dark—
or frightened by
Heat-lightning, a lost child sobbing among
Rocks, birdcalls—

Soprano

Then sit down and cry!
And now this talk reminds me of New England,
My Aunt who kept Dead Passions in a cage,
Embalmed canaries: one she called 'Emerson,'

The other was 'Thoreau'; she said both died
For love of 'Emily.' She could imagine
They were singing 'songs and snatches,'
Words she had heard and thought they sounded pretty;
Sometimes she said the birds were just herself
Waking with Uncle Henry in the morning
To see sunlight on snow—room blind with light
And warm—but that was very long ago,
Something remembered; they were foolish young,
And scarcely knew each other.
                                        I think
That you imagine what you can't hear,—hear things
You think you should.

                        Baritone

                        This is an intermission.
I feel an intermission in the air,
Everything in deeper silence than before.

(The backstage floodlight brightens.)

                        Soprano

Up there I see hands waving, people leaving;
We came too late; I knew it.
                                        Someone is taking
The big applause. Not us. I'm getting lonely.

(The floodlight is switched off.)

                        Basso

At this hour, observations are uncertain.

(The stage darkens.)

Baritone

It is odd to feel that music was not played,
But acted, talked about in wilted fragments
Of an overture and faintly heard.

Soprano

I heard nothing!

Baritone

I heard *you*, but we did not come for that;
We came to make ourselves forget the world;
We wanted music—art!
                              And all new faces.
There has been no concert.

Basso

                              You are sure
That nothing happened?

Soprano

                              Yes, I'm cheated;
I'm not wanted. My arms are cold.

Basso

                              Many are always
Coming for what they expect to see, to hear.
The actual event passes in darkness, silence;
The ikon burns in noiseless fire on the wall;
The crowd before the rostrum sleeps or cheers,
Tosses its pennies at the stage and leaves.

(He lowers his voice.)

What if I tell you that this spot is where
White Daphne changed to laurel?
                              And here is night,
A waiting pastoral silence in the sky—
The Great Wain turns within a crown of light.

Beyond the Pyramid:
Heard in the Protestant Cemetery

For Count Umberto Morra

The curtain rises on the Protestant Cemetery near Porta San Paolo in a suburb of Rome. To the extreme left there is a view of the Pyramid of Cestius, and in the foreground among rough grasses and striped Roman violets, Keats's headstone with its half-strung lyre in bas-relief faces the audience. Center stage to the extreme right shows the remains of the Servian Wall which are overgrown with grasses and form a series of terraces where headstones and memorial plaques grow with irregular profusion among vines and faded wreaths. The time is late afternoon in August. A light, drifting rain is falling, yet the sky behind the Pyramid shows signs of clearing. An undersized girl of twelve in a ragged print cotton dress enters from the left. She is quickly followed by a tall young man, an American tourist with a guidebook in his right hand.

Girl

(In a high treble voice pronouncing words slowly as if memorized and with forced clarity.)

Pyramid of Cestius. Five lire please.
Five lire, ten lire, fifteen lire. More, more—
I must go home. More lire.

(She looks up at the young man, grins and extends a thin right hand into which he counts and places four five-lira notes. She turns and runs across stage to the right, suddenly halts, then quickly climbs the terraces of the Wall, selects a seat on a grave,

*turns, settles her back against a headstone beneath a branch of a
thin-leaved olive tree which shelters her from the rain.)*

Young Man

Go home; you'll get wet; you'll catch cold—
Do you hear me? Understand me? Are you crazy?

*(She shakes her head, and settles herself with greater firmness
against the headstone. She knots the five-lira notes into a handkerchief, then relaxes, head tilted back facing the audience.)*

Young Man

Go home, go home! You have your 'lire, lire!'

(She does not stir.)

The Roman beggar of eight centuries
Smiling to rob you through brocaded doorways,
Hands thrust through laces, velvets, silks and furs,
Their fingers sharp as steel—or among stones
As quick as cats, the Romans climb, stare, quiver,
An eye above one shoulder, glide, then fade.

(He glances upward at the motionless girl.)

She has nine lives at least—her pitch these ruins
For two hundred years.

(He consults his guidebook.)

And there's the Pyramid (the sides look dark,
Crosshatched and dark in Piranesi's ink,
Black grasses and black creatures in the weeds,
Cocked hats and turkey feathers) a black phallus

190

And white skull that stare through dust,
Weeds mounting from rich Cestius' foolish breast:
He piled these stones against the flood of darkness
That holds him now—the weeds, his days, his hours,
His heirs to greet new seasons.

(A voice calls from a plaque in the Servian Wall.)

Voice

Rosa, Rosa!

Young Man

(Glancing upward toward girl who does not stir.)

Someone is calling you—why don't you answer?

Voice

I am not calling *her.*

Young Man

    I *know* that voice,
Der alte Meister! Dead for twenty years.
I don't believe in ghosts. Impossible!

Voice

Rosa, Rosa! Come, I am here, trust me,
Rosa, *Rosa!*
    She has no will but mine,
Her ways, my ways. She is my daughter.

*(The stage grows dark. A spotlight illuminates a bronze plaque
in the Wall from which the voice speaks. There is a tearing sound*

—then sounds of falling earth and stones. Below the plaque grasses and wreaths are giving way to a door slowly being thrust open from within.)

Voice

It is my fate to walk. No shroud can hold me.
Each day I walk there are slow steps from midnight,
Half-moons in falling dust, split bones, thorns, wires,
The fallen crossbeams, bolts—the cobwebs scratch:
This damned Wall drives its face against my lips—
Roots through eye-sockets, and between the teeth
Torn silks, gold filings, silver filigree,
Between the ribs, a crystal amulet
Sways, glitters, drops. It is a frozen dial
To tell what? Time?
                    I've lost it
Where no loss matters—except the spirit.

(Lightly with a short laugh.)

Impossible! Of course I am all that.

(Through the opened door in the Wall an old man steps, brushing dust from his shoulders. He whips a white handkerchief from his left sleeve and dusts well polished boots. As the stage grows lighter, he is revealed as one dressed in high Edwardian fashion; he has a neatly clipped white beard and wears light grey flannels and highly polished gold-rimmed eyeglasses. He has thin white hair and is bareheaded.)

I am not a ghost, but spirit—heard, seen, felt,
Inviolate trick of the senses—and unwilled
By them.
            And if you see me, I am here—

Life in broom-flower, delicate thrust through rock:
You need not look at it or me.

(His left arm drops to his side.)

                              You've heard me, Rosa;
Now, take my hand.
                    All living is precarious
In time or out of it—
                    dangerous in Nature:
Roots break through cellars, upheaving floors,
Trees' branches reach out leaves through dormer windows
And roofs lift in a rush of vines and grasses,
Everything human crushed, broken, swept away
In life transforming life: acres of locusts
Where once a growing wheat field tossed its waves—
Nature returns to Nature.
                    But the spirit?
Myself alive to call my daughter Rosa?
You do not see her because you never met her,
A blue-eyed child with a Victorian name:
I kept her young, dressed in white frocks, black slippers,
Ribbons in her hair, hair flowing at her shoulders,
Herself my voice, my art, my Galatea,
I, her Pygmalion, leaning over her,
The patient teacher, careful, gentle father
Waking great music in her veins, my spirit—
She never lost me—she as the half-strung lyre
On that headstone waiting my breath, my lips
To stir its strings.

Young Man

        I half remember
So long ago—an all night walk, a forest,
The lake beside me in moon-mask of waves,

March air among bleak branches and torn skies
Streaked with metallic light across the morning.

Voice

Yes. Was that all?

Young Man

      I heard a child's voice chanting:
'Birth-gendering Venus, mistress of gods and men,
Your stairways of the sea mount shores of laughter,
And where you walk sweet-smelling flowers rise—
All earth awakens in your blessed light . . .'
That was Lucretius, or inspired by him,
Yet when I reached the place, the child was gone—
A usual empty path between bare trees.

Voice

That was my Galatea—my touch of sin
At loving her too much, too much temptation
To make her oversweet—the vessel filled too full,
And trembling at its brim, it overturned—
Then childish chatter and blank eyes and tears,
A helpless hand in mine—O but her voice!
The half-strung lyre! Yet she cannot die,
Nor I.

(Lightly, changing his tone.)

      In spring I wear a jonquil,
Not wilting violets, but jonquil staring,
Admiring itself in every mirror,

In swollen iris of a bird, a glass of wine,
Bright shop-window, or tilted shaving-glass—
If golden-naked, jonquil's in high fashion,
The graceful fisher-boy at a deep pool.

Young Man

One would have thought to find you in *your* country,
Not here.

Voice

     O yes! *My* country!
You mean my birthplace, not the place of being—
A weathered, darkened farmhouse and locked doors,
The midnight cry of birth and drifting snows,
The cradle rocking, 'endlessly rocking . . .'
To what frontier?
              Not mine. My country
Is what I make my country—where I live,
Habit for the spirit—not in Purgatory—
Not lost that way—nor is my pasture
The quiet discourse of Elysian Fields,
Pale shade embracing shade, the pastel lovers,
Beatitudes in sheeps' wool and sad eyes—
Rather the simultaneous rush of Rome,
Of rifts in timelessness: the blood-red comet
Behind the laurel wreath—Caesar, Il Duce,
Porta del Popolo where a black tree
Holds Nero's ghost within its magic branches—
Is he a raven or a crow?
           And Juno's temple,
Maria in Aracoeli.
           In golden dust, in light,
In fire that burns weak hopes, all grief away.

195

(From a breast pocket he produces a cigarette-case and lighter which he extends to the Young Man who steps back.)

Young Man

(Startled into rudeness.)

NO! . . . I beg your pardon!

Voice

(He selects a cigarette; lights it with a flourish, repockets his cigarette-case and lighter.)

Vanity again! The fault of charm. I keep small vices,
Evading death, hell's darkness.

(He raises his right hand as though holding a small cup.)

            I lift a coffee cup
Against the night! The cup is frail enough,
Yet catches a reflection from the sun.
Rosa, my hand!

(To the Young Man.)

         Bring that far girl to me!

(The Young Man mounts the terraces, presses a five-lira note into the girl's hand and leads her to the center of the stage.)

Young Man

(Smiling as though introducing her.)

The lire-girl—she's rich—she's Cestius' daughter!

196

No. Neither his, nor mine.
                              Strip off her rags
She's Botticelli's Flora: impudent chin,
A pert, all-knowing smile, an immortality
More durable than ours— Venus, her goddess
Of the Primavera and that ancient dance
That dark Lucretius knew.

(Sternly.)

                              Rosa, take Flora's hand;
I shall not hold you—the utter death, not yet—
There is a life beyond that Pyramid,
Seasons beyond the Aprils that we know—
Hope vanishes, then fears.

(He points to the bronze plaque on the Servian Wall above the door from which he made his entrance.)

                              Behind that plaque,
My bones—cry, 'Ave, ave!'
                              O let them rest in dust—
The spirit does not.
                      Porta del Popolo
My walk through spring and summer up the Corso:
Rienzi fallen in a golden cloud,
The smell of blood, dogs barking,
Mussolini hanged by the heels in Milan;
His ghost is here. And this is hell? Perhaps.
Nothing by halves. I raise my coffee cup
Where Petrarch wears bronze laurels as a crown—
Laura in excelis seen in the waiting faces
Of Roman girls who sit at apértifs—
Himself a golden flame where lovers meet.

(With left hand at her side as though clasping an invisible hand.)

I must go home.

(She runs left and off stage. The stage grows dark, then lights again. The old man has vanished and the door below his plaque has closed.)

Voice

(From the plaque on which a spotlight plays.)

> 'Home, home,' and 'home' again,
> An immortality!
> The Pyramid smokes
> In the wind and is about to fall—stones shift
> And polished bronze grows thin,
> Turns green in earth to nourish hungry lizards.
> The spirit walks until all clocks unwind—
> Alone? Perhaps.
> And where are my frontiers?

Young Man

In Rome? . . . in timelessness? Why count the years!

Dottissimi Signori: Giacomo Leopardi

Due cose belle ha il mondo
Amore e morte.

—LEOPARDI

Listen to hidden music: Morte ti chiama
Where Giacomo sits, the sleepless spirit
With a flickering tongue, the spiral flame
In sunlit heat that rises: Morte ti chiama
From where? From the heart of noon,
From Iron Table, from Chair that waits
In fiery light pouring its ceaseless arrows,
Morte ti chiama in an empty square.

In divine light Giacomo is not human:
Both more and less than human in the sun,
His breath in fire, unwanted, always there,
Wraith in a blue coat under a black hat,
Dottissimi signori sipping ices,
Little tree toad that does not weep, but spits,
Or priest or devil in his glancing smile—
Here, here or there, or there and gone—

His beatific smile that slips between
Kisses of lovers in a latticed window
Or behind shutters in a shop, his breath
Between their lips—suddenly, 'Il Gobbo!
Morte ti chiama!' in a whispered echo.

Giacomo Leopardi, poet, was born at Recanati, 1798, and
died at Naples, 1837. Gloss.: Dottissimi Signori roughly
equals Gentleman-Scholar; Monte ti chiama, death calls
you; Il gobbo, the hunchback; Fanny Targione was
Leopardi's 'Aspasia.'

No, he has not touched them, yet his smile
Entered the room and vanished through closed doors,
And far away, a whining violin:

Morte ti chiama, voice of the damned
Who heard a farm girl sing her heart away,
A burning virgin in an upland meadow,
Saw Luciola leaning from her window,
Blessed them like a spent priest, and saw them fade
Into the sunlit visions of the soul,
The fragile broom-flower through ruined walls,
Morte ti chiama in their childhood's summer.

Where Giacomo runs through Recanati,
Flying from cries of children through the streets,
'Il Gobbo, Gobbo-toad, make music for us,
Crow like a leaping monkey on a stick,'
Among stones flying, see Il Gobbo run,
More stones that fly than arrows at Sebastian—
These pierce the cassock striking at the heart—
Morte ti chiama through Il Gobbo's flight.

And after them, the Fanny Targione
Who cries, 'Il mio gobbetto, ah, my cat,
My devil who's my blue-eyed marmoset,
My little cupid with his broken back,
Who brings me roses on a winter evening,
His forked tongue at my breast: take him away!
And as he leaves the house, sweep out the parlor;
The devil sweats in sulphur where he walks.'

Morte ti chiama chiming where he turns:
No, he is not of earth: he is of the cloisters
Of the far Diana in her silver net,
Or of the flame that burns within the sun.

He is of their being, careless of the world,
All cold, all heat, the fever at his throat,
And cannot sleep, nor any grave his bed,
He walks abroad and steps his way to Naples—

To noon at Naples among brisk whores and thieves,
Among the lost and laughing: Morte ti chiama
Crying around him through blind heat and shade.
Beyond midday, the sun falls to the waters,
Beyond midnight, the setting of the moon
Into a timeless noon—his unseen presence
Restless at empty Chair, at waiting Table,
And from his broken tomb: Morte ti chiama.

Flight to the Hebrides

The *Tourists' Day* lurched through steep, grey-haired waters:
Hundreds of passengers, heads, eyes, thousands of gulls
Sweeping the air above them, diving, rising, swaying;
They'd tear fish from the sea alive, bread from the throat—
Was that an eye plucked out? No. That was a cut of the wind,
The knife flying through air, the salt-edged, caustic spray.

Yet it was very close, a near try at almost death,
A sliding deck, the rail, not over, but against the rail—
There, across the sea, the waiting, green-streaked islands:
The great-eyed caves where waters foam and flounder,
And over them dark hills and darker skies that break
In sunburst flashed through cloud, half-rain, half-lightning.

Below decks, brass-bound stairs in smoke-closed heat,
The pale man with a drink, the portholes shuttered.
'That was very close,' a woman said, 'How is your heart?'
Hand on his shoulder, 'Do you need another?'
                                        'What,
A heart or drink? Give me another drink.'
                                        'They almost
Got you, didn't they dear—that time.'
                                        'Not now, but later,
Not the damned gulls, I mean the others who look like gulls;
Above my head, they follow me in clouds. Murder makes murder,
Even if you wear gloves: blood grows in blood; it spills and stains.
You won't tell? Women always tell; they always tell; they weep.'

'But you didn't do it; you mustn't say you did. Here's drink—
O drink my love to sleep! You're ill again, but you'll escape.
Here are the islands and the caves; you'll slip ashore
Into the waves and the wild Hebrides.'

'No one can lift me,
Carry me from this room. Did you take the gun? If I don't
Go out, I'm safe, they can't tell a sick man to leave the ship.
Do you see the gulls? They're coming: I can't get away,
Not even from you. They can't lift me from this place
To hide where I need not hide in a cave to drown—'
'But you said you would smile and slowly walk ashore.'

'Not to those islands—dark, lit by a crazy sky,
Hills, water to cover me where bones float to the sand,
Not there, naked to wind, sea, sun, moon, stars, bats, fishes—
I need a room to wear—heat, fire—then they can take me
Through a locked door in a hotel in bed between the sheets
Behind *The Daily Mail, News of the World, The Times*—not God.
And now, you're crying. You'll tell, you'll tell—half-lies,
Won't leave until you see me flat and dead. That's what you want.
You're another gull, white breasts and pink-rimmed eyes,
And a heart-shaped, round-teared stare. Do you hear the gulls
Make shore, feet flying above us? Take your God-haunted, God-
    feared,
God-damned islands. This room is mine, and I'll sit here,
Back to the city: light lit above the bar, deep smells,
Hope gone, you won't dare leave me. That's home: a windowed
    street,
A chair, a table, a bed, or night, or day—and voices.
They can take me then. One step at a time. In a room
At night, cars parked. You can hear them. *They!*'

ALLEGORIES & PARABLES

—for Marya Zaturenska

Three Allegories of Bellini

I: *Virtue and the Gorgon*

We keep the door locked
Because the picture in that room,
The tall Bellini,
Takes hold of night:
It shows a naked woman,
An awkward creature
With an ungainly face
And female, half-dressed
Cupids at her feet—
One beating a toy drum.

Bang! Bang! And yet no noise.
One cupid has a horn—
Silence again. The woman
Points one finger at a glass
That has a Gorgon's head
Reflected in it—
What was once beautiful
A sight of horror—
The greatest terror
In its loss of beauty.

The woman is secure
In awkwardness:

Plain, naked as she is,
Shameless in virtue
On pedestal, points where
Snakes writhe and spit
In a grey Gorgon's hair.

She warns and takes her
Second best as best—
No loss, nor harm
Could ever change her face,
Nor move her. The toy drum
Soundless. The horn
Unheard. Her lack of grace
Supreme. The mediocre
Triumph stands at rest.

The picture looms at night:
It would be untrue
To say the picture walks—
No naked footfalls heard
Across the floor;
Passionless virtue
Does not pace dark hours;
Half-damned it stands
In anterooms of hell—
Shall I unlock the door?

II: *Amoretti and Venus*

Love, love! Turn to the fair-
Haired woman in a boat
In a rough sea—two Amoretti,
Ugly little beasts,
Drowning at her side—

Yet two are saved:
One standing at the prow
Blows a short trumpet.
She balances a globe
On her left knee—
It is the world,
Continents, seas, rivers,
And countless creatures
At which she stares;
She is Mistress Venus.

The boat is thin, is frail—
God save us!—a gondola!
Balance precarious
Between lust and hope,
Between sea and air,
Waves, waves are rising,
And through the skies
An angry flush of sunset—
All may go down with it.

Is the child with the trumpet
A gondolier?
No, no, he is in the prow:
He blows his trumpet.
His cheeks are filled with wind;
He will be the last survivor—
He does not steer.

They are still riding—
One does not call it sailing—
Through seas, through tempest.
The trumpet blowing
Is sign of victory.
Two Amoretti drowned

Is not her concern.
She holds the world;
It is her obsession—
Should seas prevail
Is another matter.

She is Mistress Venus;
The last storm may not come;
She is not wise;
She has been known to fail—
She has been called a whore
As well as goddess,
And at her breast, another Amoretto—
Balance again!
Will they reach a farther shore?
And 'Love, love, love!'
Cries the shrill trumpet.

III: *Aquarium*

And did you see them pass?—
No, they are here:
Fluorescent, double faces
Each to each in the green glass
Behind the bar, leaning
As if forever
Through the mirror.

They are above the earth,
Not quite in air:
It is said they give the place
An atmosphere.

They are not lost;
They have come to float
Before the waiting,
Watchful dinner hour,
To echo whispers
In a sliding smile,
To look as if to hear
An answer fall
From a drooped eyelid
As dew from frost
That holds a secret
In an ice-cooled grail.

Note the slow gesture:
I mean the woman
With the saffron scarf:
It is as if her arms
Had changed to vines,
As though they drifted up
Through salt-green waters.
She is among the late,
The last arrivers:
She has confessed
For over thirty years
That her best friends are
Always taxi-drivers.

Although the group
Has travelled everywhere,
Each place they visit
Is a café at four,
And where they choose to sit,
A pale green mirror.

There is a mystery
Painted by Bellini
Of figures standing
On a marble terrace:
Women and men—and in
The foreground—children,
All looking into space
As if to Nowhere,
Each face preoccupied—
And all look sad.

As if to clear
That curious mystery,
Someone decided
To call it, 'Purgatory.'

And yet the figures
Floating through pale glass
Are not unhappy;
They are busy talking
As though they lived
In Palaces of Hell,
Excitement in each eye,
Each word a gesture.
They neither rise nor fall;
Their waters ripple
Deeper than sound is heard,
Or rivers flow:
They are still here;
Each born to haunt
The places that they know.

Homage to Utopia

'If I had the time,' said MacMurry O'Keefe,
'I would change this cold world
To perpetual summer:
The sun in the sky
And each flower in leaf,
Each tree a green shade
And the grasses grown wild
Where each human face
Is a happy Newcomer.'

'If I had the brains,' and he emptied his glass,
'War would vanish away
As the snow in the street
Then black Crime and Despair
Like their shadows would pass
Into light of noonday
On the waves of the sea
And the Furies of Night
Would fly into retreat.

'If I had the heart,' and he paid for his drink,
'Peace would flow from my veins
Like their rivers of blood
And no creature run mad
With the effort to think:
There'd be no breaks and sprains
In the flutter of brains—
But my friends would be gone
And myself would be dead.'

Said MacMurry O'Keefe as he walked out the door,
'Nobody on earth

Would be here anymore
Which might not be a curse,
But a cosmic relief.'
Said MacMurry O'Keefe.

The Wilds of Saint Antony

'On earth there are devils
That breathe, through the air
And eat through the petals
Of lilies and roses
In triples and doubles:
They slip through my whiskey
And bitter my beer.
        They're here and not here—
        And as quick as a thief—'
        Said MacMurry O'Keefe.
'When Saint Antony sat
All alone in the park,
Though they half-pleased and charmed him,
Amazed and alarmed him,
He frightened at things
That looked naked and wild
As he saw their white bodies
Flash by in the dark.
        They spoiled his refinement
        And filled him with grief—'
        Said MacMurry O'Keefe.
'The worst of the troubles
That fall through the mind
Are here and not here,—
Could you say they were there?
For they ride round the clock
And they sail through the air
Till I dream them in heaven
And face them in hell
Where doctors console me

And say I'm not well—
> Then I'm wrecked like a yacht
> On a blind coral reef—'
> Said MacMurry O'Keefe.

The Teachings of Saint Jerome

Jerome sought truth and knew the art of teaching;
Soon his reward was meeting Roman wives
Who sat before him in his grassy cave,
Humble, yet with raised breasts and restless eyes.

Their amber-studded ears could not retain
Sky-riding Plato, nor strict Origen,
Starry Plotinus, careful Cicero—
The Saint's great learning was a wraith of words.

The women gazed at him and gave him money;
He left them staring, naked in their beds—

Jerome stormed eastward to a friendless desert,
A blasted hell-raised plain beneath the moon:
There he unearthed a heathenish black skull,
And later, snared and hypnotized a lion.

The skull received his teachings gratefully
And bared its teeth whitely at life, at death;
The Saint, inspired by hope, struck at the lion,
Thrust out his eyes and spoke to him in Greek:

First dressed his wounds, then taught him rhetoric.
He grew to love the beast, nor thought of women—

Orpheus

Suddenly the world was Autumn's afternoon:
His voice went shrill, and as he raised his head,
He felt the frost of winter in his hair.

His very nostrils caught the smell of snow,
And in the eyes of creatures walled around him,
He saw his own eyes darken into fear.

The wind was full of leaves.
                              He saw beasts scatter
To take the way of beasts through rocks and caves,
Darkness to midnight and their city gone

That had been hill-treed temples of his music.
Where were his birds?
                              He saw them fluttering
From trees above him, circling naked boughs

Into the sky as though their wings had known
That deathless music flies like hope to heaven,
Streams of the Sun returning to their source.

Only the blood-billed, eager Hawk would wait—
Till the entire forest filled with blood,
Hunter and hunted in a ceaseless race,

Nor could he climb his way back to the Sun.

He heard the women's cries.
                              They could take him now
As branches torn from trees. He saw them come—
His body was an empty martyrdom.

Siesta Navona

Piazza Navona: behind a stream of light
The fountain playing. Sit down where roof and walls
Make the noon shadow.

Sleep, sleep: a dark hand falls across the forehead,
And shutters close in deeper shades of sleep.

In narrow shadow one hears moonlit waters,
One sees the changeable sirens of the fountain
Rise with green hair,

The clinging waters falling from their sides,
Their arms, their lips held in a white embrace
On shores of darkness.

The Piazza empty: a curtained door, a table,
A forgotten cloak, a chair—the moment waits.

As air sways open into endless sky
Only the fountain plays in golden light—

And from his chariot Young Apollo steps
To walk the streets of his reconquered city.

The Chinese Garden

*Near the city of Washington, D.C., there is
a Chinese Garden. Few visit it; the place
seems singularly deserted and remote.*

O yes, the Chinese Garden! Do you remember
Sun beating behind clouds? One felt the air
Shaken by streams of yellow light through aether,
And yet late summer stillness in each turn
Of paths that ran between the fading grasses,
The well-deep, glassy pool, and the damp smell,
And clouded light around us everywhere—
The half-lit madness we can never cure.

You see them now! I mean the water lilies,
White petals open as a China cup
Rising above the surface of a tray:
They are here—just out of reach—and there, the water,
The half-light in far corners of the park,
Trees fallen around it through the pale arbutus.
Do you feel the grey light at the farthest clearing
Thrusting as snow against plate glass, then gone?

Beneath the cloud-white lilies, hairy roots,
Invisible lips that breathe the cool well water
Wavering in darkness down to dreamless sleep:
The streams to walk below the net of grasses
That close above the ripples of the soul.

There were no signs to warn us: 'Walks ill-tended,
The bridges gone beneath the deeper grasses—'

Reach toward the lilies? Not that afternoon.
If one were tempted to lean out that far? ...
No, no, not now! No one would dare to hear us.
'The water has turned black.' We turned away:
It was like leaving a forbidden city,
Earth falling away behind us into darkness:
We heard a woman cry, 'But O the flowers,
Where are the flowers? The beautiful white flowers!'

Gifts of the Age

The sky hung cloudless for ninety days,
May into August: the sun's golden aether,
The moon's broad river of pouring light
Tremulous in air. I come with presents:
Striped Roman violets and blood-red cut
Carnations—and from another climate
Within a bird cage, watchful marmosets—
All gifts grown from moist grasses, split
Granite, or from difficult places where
No life seems to stir, where earth is
Empty as the plateau of a beggar's hand.

I bring you these: violets, carnations,
Marmosets, the cage that holds them, each
Incomplete without the other. Violets
Wilt in an hour, fade into colors of dust,
Carnations, dipped in water, endure a week,
But marmosets, being both wild and tame,
Wake and sleep fitfully, replenished by
Shreds of corn, by flies and beetles. They
Have been known to live ten, twenty years,
Careless of those who tend them. Violets,
Carnations are of the sun. When the moon's

Lost behind eyelids closed in sleep, from
Deepest shade the marmosets arrive. One
Sees their faces between leaves, crevices,
Between the bars, grave faces of small boys,
Speechless and docile, as though each age,

219

Golden, or silver, stone, iron, brass were
Unfit for comment, or tedious rehearsal.
The violets droop, the carnations breathe
Fragrance to the sun, the pouring moon.
The cage opens its door to midnight silence;
It is as though the walls of our room were
Vines, as though lintel and shelf were trees,
As though forever marmosets were there
Above the dark, climbing through cloudless air.

Goethe Aetat. 83: Eckermann Speaks:

The cold day waking and March wind against us—
There, there I saw him at an open door,
A shaft of Sun within an empty portal,
The old man looking as he must have been
A half century ago.
                              I was conscious only
That his body shone beneath a blue-lined cloak,
That his limbs moved as with the quickened lightness
Of white invisible fires.
                              'I have come from sleep,'
He said, 'shaking long winters from me,
Eons of chaos filled with blood-stained comets
And falling moons, black tempests and grey floods,
No stars, but nights with storm-ringed mountain-tops
Where lightning flared green arrows among clouds.'
He spread his luminous hands and smiled at us:
'The while I slept, I heard a statesman say,
Politics are Destiny. He vanished in defeat,
And after him, I heard sleek magpies chatter,
Politics are Poetry, and there I saw
A coiled snake eat them, and I heard boughs fall.'
'Let the Years sleep,' he said, 'in that locked room
Behind me, in the dwindling shadows
Of an unmade bed, in sheets, in crevices
Of floor and wall.
                              Today we breathe the Sun
Raised through the skies, that Persian draught of heaven.'
That was the last I heard.
                              He had disappeared:
The world was Spring, a flowering equinox—
Behind him came white violets in the grass.

If It Offend Thee . . .

'I confess I would rather stand out for posterity in a hideous silhouette. . . .
There happened to be the most innocent kind of party . . . at a country house
. . . at which there was a friend of my childhood that I had not seen for
years. . . . I invited the gentleman to step out on the lawn, and there I beat
him with a stick. . . . The next thing I remember is returning late at night to
my room. . . . There was a hard-coal fire burning brightly . . . I . . . plunged
the left hand deep in the blaze . . . and held it down with my right hand . . .
I said to myself, "This will never do." '
—M. A. De Wolfe Howe: JOHN JAY CHAPMAN AND HIS LETTERS

'This will not do,' he said, and thrust his left hand into the coals
        of the fire.
'This will not do . . . "if it offend thee" . . .' he kneeled to thrust it
        deeper; he could not feel pain,
But felt the darkness fill the room behind him. He had awaked
        from black sleep closed around him,
And saw his left hand shine in sin: it had struck down someone,
        perhaps an enemy, perhaps a friend.
' "If it offend thee . . ." ' That luminous face had disappeared,
        even the smile; the face was like his own.
'This will not do,' he cried, and the charred fingers
        cracked between the coals;
The right hand held the left arm firm: it was strange enough
        that he could feel no pain,
Only the darkness in the night behind him: somewhere the enemy
        lay in the brushes, behind the night.
It had been a cold room, but now warm, the fire glowing. He had
        slipped off his jacket before he slept
And heat leaped in the shadows on floor, on ceiling. The fire
        opened its eyes into his eyes.
'This will not do . . .' unless he enter the fire to know
        the greater heat, the rise, the fall of flames.

'If I go maimed,' he thought, 'I have struck it off; I shall not
              be utterly dead, but living like
A living shade within the fire: damned, but alive in the heart
              of the fire, to destroy the hand to make
Myself alive to live forever within the flames. There,' he withdrew
              the hand. It was nearly gone, but flesh
              remained;
It would not utterly disappear: 'This will not do,' he said. He had
              best go out. The room was cold and pain
              began.
He covered his left shoulder with a jacket; the hand was hidden,
              black as a snake, beneath it. He would ride—
If he could walk from the door down to the street—through elm-
              tossed Cambridge to an all-night clinic,
He would look like a soldier, drunk, in need of repair and a last
              straight drink. And the hand?
Even if struck off, what had been a hand would wear a glove. It
              would conceal a finger pointed at dark earth,
At earth, not fire, and it would say, 'This will not do.'

Suburban Hostel: Hudson River View

In blazing white above green-terraced lawns,
Grass cut as smartly as an actor's beard,
The Nursing Home stands clear—
                                        Perfect blue skies:
Narcissi, daffodil, the strict carnation,
All prizes of the cheerful gardener's art,
The gate locked fast between white lilac hedges.

Snakes, weasels, lizards, rabbits, mountain-cats
Are warned to keep away. Some are shot down,
Others are gelded, trapped to train as pets.

Down a brisk clearing where the golf course travels,
And more impervious to hope's mischance
Than swifter, less blind, more intelligent
Ancestors of his name, a white-washed deer
Raises his antlers in cast-iron quiet.
He is more artful than his natural brothers—
For look! a child has painted a red house,
A purple-eyed sunflower on his right flank,
And on his left, another hand spelled out,
AMY LOVES RICHARD 1924—
Such artifacts survive the trental summers.

2

Up where The Nursing Home unfolds its whiteness,
A starched girl guides a wheel chair with one hand,
Consults her watch and slowly reads a chart:
"Patient 15 believes his room a cell,
His bed a grave, sets fire to his mattress,

Will not play golf or bridge, refuses hobbies,
Nor paints, nor draws, nor hopes to drive a car,
Simulates deafness, talks of 'inner life,'
A stubborn case who smiles and never weeps,
Seems happy, yet remote—a sign of danger."
The girl rereads her watch, yawns, sighs, lights up
A cigarette—
    Then suddenly a cry—
And toward an oval pool, not fit for bathing,
Five male attendants race the garden paths.
Did anyone escape?
      Was that a patient?
It could not be a bird or water lily.
Murder, rebirth?
      Five strong attendants
Unroll a canvas over the drained pool,
And what is there will wait, nor creep toward light.

"Reap, reap, reap, reap," the frogs sing through the night.

On a Celtic Mask by Henry Moore

The burnished silver mask hangs in white air,
The eyes struck out, the lips raised in a smile:
Where eyes had been, the hawk-winged Hebrides,
Tall, weeping waves against their friendless shores,

Rain in small knives that cut the flesh away,
And Sun the sword that flashes from the sky:
Sea-lion-headed creatures stalk these islands,
And breed their young to stand before their graves.

A crying Magdalen sings from her grotto,
Precarious life-in-death between the waters—
None see her breasts, flushed limbs and winding hair—
The women hear her in the new moon's madness.

The Saints? That's where they came—Iona!
The burning Saints—charred bones. I saw the green
Grass-heaped and broken naves of a stone abbey,
Graves, graves and salt-cased kings beneath the ruins:

Island of wave-washed islands, as a jewel
Is set in bronze and salt-green blackened silver:
After shipwreck, the lure of peace and haven,
Goat-path and thorn, the walk where once Saint Bridget,

Bride of Mayflowers in a savage pasture,
Turned grey-green eyes to face the swords, the fires,
Spoke in bird-voices and gave grace to poets,
Then sought her Holy Cave, but stepped toward heaven.

Some say that Irish souls turn into lemmings,
And rush the violent seas that guard Iona.